T0339502

The Socratic Oath for Teachers

What makes a good teacher? In 1991, Hartmut von Hentig attempted to answer this question when he first formulated a 'Socratic oath' for the profession, and it is a question which remains relevant today. In *The Socratic Oath for Teachers*, Klaus Zierer revisits and reframes the concept of a teacher's oath while also addressing challenges currently facing our societal developments in recent didactic–methodological research and fresh perspectives on the goals of the teaching profession. Referencing Socrates throughout, this short think piece proposes a professional oath for teachers that at its core is fully committed to the successful education and well-being of students.

Drawing upon key research and his own experiences within education, Zierer answers the following questions, establishing how a professional oath may support teachers:

- What is a professional oath, and what can it do?
- What characterises teacher professionalism?
- What can be understood by teacher attitudes? Why are they crucial for a successful professional oath?
- Why is Socrates suitable as a guarantor for a professional oath of teachers?
- Why is a renewal of the Socratic Oath necessary?
- For whom is an oath necessary, and what must it contain?

In this fascinating work, Klaus Zierer explores the principles and goals of the teaching profession and formulates theoretically sound and empirically validated principles of successful teaching. This is an essential read for any teacher, senior leader, policy maker, educationalist, or researcher who wants to learn more about what makes a good teacher.

Klaus Zierer, a German educationalist and professor of the School of Education at the University of Augsburg since 2015, is considered to be the leading Hattie expert in the German-speaking world. Previously, he was Professor of Educational Science at the Carl von Ossietzky University of Oldenburg and an elementary school teacher from 2004 to 2009. He has co-authored the successful books *10 Mindframes for Visible Learning* and *Visible Learning Insights* alongside John Hattie. In addition, he has extensively contributed to education policy debates and is considered one of the most influential school educators in Germany.

The Socratic Oath for Teachers

Klaus Zierer

Routledge
Taylor & Francis Group

LONDON AND NEW YORK

First published 2024
by Routledge
4 Park Square, Milton Park, Abingdon, Oxon OX14 4RN

and by Routledge
605 Third Avenue, New York, NY 10158

Routledge is an imprint of the Taylor & Francis Group, an informa business

British Library Cataloguing-in-Publication Data
A catalogue record for this book is available from the British Library

ISBN: 978-1-032-57422-6 (hbk)
ISBN: 978-1-032-57419-6 (pbk)
ISBN: 978-1-003-43928-8 (ebk)

DOI: 10.4324/9781003439288

Typeset in Times New Roman
by Apex CoVantage, LLC

Contents

'Let him that would move the world first move himself'

Socrates

As a teacher, I commit myself to directing all my feelings, thoughts, and actions in my profession towards the well-being of the children entrusted to my care.

To the children, I commit myself

- *to challenge and encourage each child according to his or her potential and level of development,*
- *not to leave any child behind or write them off, no matter what the reasons are,*
- *to take the failure of the children entrusted to me over and over again as an occasion for new ways of teaching,*
- *to see mistakes as an opportunity, not a flaw,*
- *to set challenges in the educational process so that under- and overstraining do not occur,*
- *to seek, pick up, and awaken motivations,*
- *to enter into dialogue again and again, to give and receive feedback, to ask questions, and to listen,*
- *to assign subjects a serving function in the educational process,*
- *to address and stimulate all areas of the personality,*
- *to inspire confidence in the world and in oneself and to make it visible on a daily basis,*
- *to understand and shape the classroom and the school as a welcoming place,*
- *to provide an atmosphere and relationship that is respectful, free of fear, and educationally effective, and*
- *to stand up for the physical, mental, and spiritual integrity of the children entrusted to me.*

To the parents, I commit myself

- *to communicate on an equal footing and to establish an educational partnership,*
- *to understand the educational process of the children as a common task,*
- *not only to be prepared to talk to them on a regular basis but also to actively seek contact with them, and*
- *to take their assessments of the children's educational success and progress seriously and to combine them with their own views.*

To my colleagues, I commit myself

- *to share my experiences in education and teaching and to use them as a basis for collegial professionalization,*
- *to share and reflect together on the mistakes made every day,*
- *to reflect back on successful moments in school and give mutual recognition, and*
- *to allow everyone to have their own individual perspective on school and teaching while working towards a shared vision.*

To the educational public, I commit myself

- *to accept the education mission and to implement it at all times,*
- *not only to impart knowledge and skills but to focus on and promote all areas of the personality,*
- *to subordinate all subjects to the well-being of the child and thus to the educational mission,*
- *to be loyal, but not blindly so, to official requirements,*
- *to implement everything that is in the best interests of the child and to reject everything that is contrary to the best interests of the child,*
- *to critically question and, if necessary, publicly accuse and reject any interests and demands on schools and teaching that are not primarily in the best interests of the child, and*
- *to give a voice in public discourse to children and their right to education.*

To society, I commit myself

- *to see respect for the dignity of the human being as the basis and goal of school and teaching,*
- *to teach the principles of our democracy and to defend them in school and in the classroom,*
- *to see school as a place for the reproduction and innovation of social values,*

- *to use my pedagogical freedom to place current issues at the centre of the school day, and*
- *to be not only reactive but also proactive towards the further development of our society.*

To myself, I commit

- *to justify my actions at all times, to discuss them critically and constructively, and to reflect on them conscientiously,*
- *to regularly develop my professional, pedagogical, and didactic competencies,*
- *to regularly reflect on my professional attitudes, and*
- *to always perform my function as a role model to the best of my knowledge and belief.*

I confirm what has been said by my willingness to be measured at all times against the standards that emanate from this commitment.

1   Why this book?

We spend about 15,000 hours of our lives in school and are taught by an average of 50 teachers.[1] Yet we remember only a handful of them for a lifetime, even though they all had the same students, the same parents, the same classrooms, the same equipment, and the same everything as everyone else. What is the secret of their success?

In this context, the words spoken by French President Emmanuel Macron at the Élysée Palace on 22 October 2020 remain unforgettable. The occasion for his speech was a memorial service for Samuel Paty.

Samuel Paty was a teacher of history and geography. He taught at the Collège du Bois-d'Aulne in Conflans-Sainte-Honorine and was 47 years old, married, and a father. After he discussed the topic of freedom of expression in class, showing a cartoon of Mohammed from the satirical magazine *Charlie Hebdo*, discussions arose in the school community sparked by parents from the Islamist camp. On 16 October 2020, Samuel Paty was beheaded in the open street by Abdullah Ansorow. This murder was the fifth Islamist assassination in France in 2020. Against this backdrop, however, Emmanuel Macron did not speak about Islamism and terrorism, as one might assume, but about successful teachers, using Samuel Paty as an example. Here are just a few excerpts from the impressive speech:[2]

> More than anything else, Samuel Paty loved books, knowledge. His apartment was a library. His finest presents were books to learn from. He loved relaying to his students and loved ones a passion for knowledge and the taste of freedom through books. . . . Samuel Paty was passionate about teaching and did it so well in several high schools, right up to the high school in Conflans-Sainte-Honorine. We all have firmly lodged in our hearts, our memories, a teacher who changed the course of our lives. You know, that primary school teacher who taught us to read, count, and have confidence in ourselves. The teacher who not only taught us a piece of knowledge but opened up a path for us through a book, through their attentiveness.

DOI: 10.4324/9781003439288-1

Samuel Paty was one of them, one of those teachers you don't forget, one of those passionate people able to spend nights learning the history of religions so he could better understand his students and their beliefs. One of those humble people who questioned themselves a thousand times. . . . Samuel Paty basically embodied the teacher Jaurès dreamed of in the letter to teachers, which has just been read out: 'firmness combined with tenderness'. He who shows the greatness of thought teaches respect and shows what civilisation is. . . . So Ferdinand Buisson's words echo back: 'To make a republican', he wrote, 'it is necessary to give every human being, no matter how young or meek, the idea that he must think on his own, that he must be faithful or obedient to no one, that it is up to him to seek truth and not receive it ready made from a teacher, guide, or leader of any sort'. 'Making republicans' was what Samuel Paty fought for.

So why was Samuel killed? Why? On Friday evening, at first I believed it to be a random act of madness, a senseless arbitrary act: another victim of gratuitous terrorism. After all, he wasn't the Islamists' main target, he was simply teaching. He wasn't an enemy of the religion they exploit: he had read the Koran; he respected his students whatever their beliefs and was interested in Muslim civilisation. No, on the contrary, that's precisely why Samuel Paty was killed. Because he embodied the Republic which comes alive every day in classrooms, the freedom that is conveyed and perpetuated in schools.

On Friday, Samuel Paty became the face of the Republic, of our determination to disrupt terrorists, to curtail Islamists, to live as a community of free citizens in our country; he became the face of our determination to understand, to learn, to continue to teach, to be free, because we will continue to do so, sir. We will defend the freedom that you taught so well, and we will strongly proclaim the concept of secularism. We will not disavow the cartoons, the drawings, even if others recoil. We will provide all the opportunities that the Republic owes all its young people, without any discrimination. We will continue, sir. France's schoolteachers, primary and secondary schoolteachers, will teach history – both its glories and its vicissitudes. We will help our students discover literature, music, all the works of the mind and soul. With all our strength, we will enjoy debate, reasonable arguments, friendly persuasion. We will love science and its controversies.

Nous continuerons, professeur!'

It's an impressive statement from a national leader in more ways than one: First, the words reveal a deep understanding that being a successful teacher is not just about knowledge and skill. What is particularly influential are the values that a teacher embodies and that drive them. Second, it is courageous to stand in front of the cameras not only of one's own nation but of the entire world and to take a stand in all clarity – for democracy and, above all, for the teaching profession.

In these situations, as someone who has been active in teacher education all my life, I squint at France and rub my eyes in amazement as to why such avowals are not to be heard in all countries of the world, for example not in Germany. On the contrary, Gerhard Schröder, then Minister President of Lower Saxony and later the ninth German Chancellor, went on record as saying that teachers were 'lazy sods'. Even though he distanced himself from his statement 25 years later, the damage had been done and remains today.[3]

Thus, this book is written primarily for teachers. It is intended to help them to accept and perform their task, which is so important for individuals and for society. In the course of a lifetime, a crisis will always arise for which the Socratic Oath can serve as a guideline. In addition, the Socratic Oath is intended to demonstrate to everyone else – learners, parents, educational administrators, and society at large – how important and multifaceted the teaching profession is while at the same time reminding them that everyone can, indeed must, make a contribution to it if a nation (like Germany) is to continue to be a nation of education.

Of course, self-commitment alone does not make for good teaching and does not create educational success on its own. This requires more, for example a certain level of equipment, a certain level of financial security, and much more still. Above all, however, it requires the activity of the learners. For education is and remains essentially an intrapersonal process, a process for which the individual is responsible. In other words, education does not mean what has been made of me but what I have made of my life.

But this also applies to the teaching profession. Its success depends crucially on the professionalism of the individual. Therefore, as true as it is that self-commitment alone cannot achieve anything, it is also true that without this self-commitment, almost everything that is possible in terms of innovations in the school system fizzles out. Whether it's reducing class sizes from 30 to 20 learners, providing millions in funding for digitalisation, introducing a new curriculum, or changing the school system, these measures always fail to succeed if the teachers are not behind them. Creating structures and strengthening people is therefore one of the most important findings of empirical educational research. After all, it is the people who bring the school system to life. Successful teacher action is a question of attitude, and that can be fixed in the form of a professional oath.

At this point, I would like to thank Andreas Breitenstein, an editor at the *Neue Zürcher Zeitung*. When I sent him my German text in February 2022, he was taken by it and made it possible for it to be published on 21 March 2022, under the title 'Was ist ein guter Lehrer?' ('What is a good teacher?'). For me, this was the start of a deeper exploration that at its core turned out to be an amalgamation of my theoretical and empirical work over the past twenty years. This led to an initial article, 'Der Sokratische Eid' ('The Socratic Oath'), published in *Pädagogische Rundschau* issue 4/2022. For this I would like to thank Univ.-Prof. apl. Dr. Birgit Ofenbach in her function as editor in chief. She agreed to publish an extension of the article as a book of the same name at Waxmann Publishing House. Much feedback followed, including approval and criticism. Both are welcome, and both are important in my endeavour to present a contemporary interpretation of the Socratic Oath. Progress in knowledge is never the preserve of an individual but is always dependent on dialogue. An initial publication of an English version followed in *Education Today* (Australia), and that was the starting point for the present book.[4] I would like to thank Beate Plugge of Waxmann Publishing House for her cooperation in transferring the rights to Taylor and Francis and also Bruce Roberts of Taylor and Francis, who has now provided me with excellent guidance in publishing several books.

Without question, a certain amount of pathos (emotional appeal) and ethos (moral appeal) always resonates in the following remarks. If one follows at this point the insight of Aristotle that these – alongside logos (consistency) – are two of the three most important aspects of a successful speech, then this is intended and indispensable, in particular for a renewal of the Socratic Oath.[5]

I would like to invite a broad public interested in education to discuss the remarks made in this book critically and constructively. Education is one of the most important fields in society as a whole. It is time that we perceived and shaped it with the appropriate seriousness.

Notes

1 Cf. Rutter, M. et al. (1980): *15 000 Stunden. Schulen und ihre Wirkung auf die Kinder.* Weilheim, and Hattie, J. & Zierer, K. (2020): *Visible Learning Unterrichtsplanung.* Baltmannsweiler, p. 295.
2 Cf. www.diplomatie.gouv.fr/en/french-foreign-policy/human-rights/freedom-of-religion-or-belief/article/national-tribute-to-the-memory-of-samuel-paty-speech-by-emmanuel-macron (retrieved on 21.03.2022).
3 Cf. www.spiegel.de/politik/deutschland/gerhard-schroeder-ueber-lehrer-doch-keine-faulen-saecke-a-3231b394-af98-4ab7-8131-e08ac1557fe0 (retrieved on 21.03.2022).
4 Cf. www.educationtoday.com.au/news-detail/Do-We-Need-a-Renewal-of-the-Socratic-Oath-5599 (retrieved on 24.02.2023).
5 Cf. Aristoteles (1999): *Rhetorik.* Stuttgart.

2 What is a professional oath, and what can it do?

Thirty years ago, Hartmut von Hentig attempted to formulate a professional oath for teachers at a time when there was no coronavirus pandemic, no climate crisis, and no Ukraine conflict and when the world seemed all right by the standards of the time.[1] He was prompted by the need for a public commitment in the face of many reforms and counter-reforms that – as in German National Socialism and the German Democratic Republic – followed uneducational points of view and did not serve the welfare of children.

Without a doubt, Hartmut von Hentig has – for many and quite understandably – gone from being the doyen of German pedagogy to a 'persona non grata' against the background of his involvement in the Odenwald School. To make it clear at this point: The sexual assaults at the Odenwald School, for which Gerold Becker, Hartmut von Hentig's life partner, was largely responsible, are an atrocity that cannot be justified. Any attempt to do so must fail because it tramples on the dignity of the children. The fact that Hartmut von Hentig,[2] of all people, has tried to do this in an amateurish way is all the more irritating because he, of all people, must know from his work in educational science that sexual assaults can usually be explained, perhaps even understood, but never justified.

What is true of the person, however, need not be true of his scientific work and the history of its reception. The 'rigorous conception of the unity of work and person', writes Jürgen Habermas, 'seems to me inadequate to the autonomy of thought and, indeed, to the general history of the reception and influence of philosophical thought'.[3] And with regard to Martin Heidegger and his active involvement in National Socialism, he formulates:

> The questionable behaviour of an author certainly casts a shadow on his work. But Heidegger's work, especially *Being and Time*, has such an eminent place in the philosophical thought of our century that it is absurd to suppose that the substance of this work could be discredited by political assessments of Heidegger's fascist involvement more than five decades later.[4]

DOI: 10.4324/9781003439288-2

This also applies – mutatis mutandis – to the person and work of Hartmut von Hentig. He can certainly damage the work through his personal activity, but he can never bring it down. If we as educational scientists were to take the rigorous (epistemological) view of the indissoluble connection between work and person at face value, even the further reading of Jean-Jacques Rousseau's *Emile* in educational science courses would be forbidden.

Thus, Hartmut von Hentig's pedagogical reflections are still innovative and inspiring today. This is especially true of the Socratic Oath as he first formulated it in 1991. In Germany, generations of teachers have grappled with it and been guided by it.[5]

Even then, Hartmut von Hentig said that an oath seemed to be lost in time and was strange for people today. Why then, of all things, do we need a professional oath for teachers? It is necessary because on the one hand, it represents a public commitment to subordinate the teacher's actions to the welfare of the child, and on the other hand, it has a protective effect against mechanisms that could hinder the exercise of the teaching profession.[6]

With these remarks, Hartmut von Hentig took up a discourse that has been conducted again and again in educational science and whose main features can be traced.[7] It is certainly remarkable that professional oaths for teachers are under discussion not only in Germany. There are several versions worldwide. The greatest controversy has arisen in the United States, where since 1863 almost two-thirds of the states have introduced and legally enshrined oaths of loyalty for teachers.[8] The Massachusetts Teachers' Oath, for example, was a loyalty oath that had been legally required for the teaching profession in Massachusetts since 1935. After major discussions about the scope of the loyalty oath, which extended into the private sphere, the law was repealed in 1967. Other current variants are, for example, the Comenius Oath in Finland,[9] the Teachers' Oath in the Philippines,[10] the Abdul Kalam Teachers' Oath in India,[11] the Teachers' Pledge in Singapore, and the Betimi i Mësuesit in Kosovo.[12]

First of all, it is necessary to clarify what an oath is in the first place for the meaning of the word 'oath' is manifold. Etymologically, it is only documented in the eighth century, but the term and thus the understanding can be found again and again in numerous circumstances since antiquity, which demonstrates its enduring significance. Thus, oaths appear in everyday language even today – for example as an oath of office; as the swearing-in ceremony of the German chancellor or the US president; as perjury, when a witness knowingly and intentionally makes a false statement; as a vow, for example in the Catholic Church when joining a religious community; or as a declaration under oath, such as for a student research paper. In each of these contexts, it is not only a matter of affirming a statement but also of committing oneself to having made that statement to the best of one's knowledge and belief and thus of bearing the consequences if one fails to fulfil that commitment for whatever reason.

The differences in the aforementioned contexts may be seen in the authority the oath taker invokes when speaking the oath. In the case of the oath of office of the German chancellor, it can be the Basic Law and thus the German people (possibly with the addition 'So help me God!') or, in the case of the vow of a religious brother, God and the religious community.

A special position within these oaths is occupied by the Hippocratic Oath, named after the ancient physician Hippocrates of Kos, because it has one of the longest histories. It is still discussed today within medical ethics and adapted to current positions (for example, abortion). Among other things, it contains obligations to protect the sick from harm and to keep patient information confidential.

A further difference in the above contexts can be seen with regard to the consequences. Whereas perjury, for example, is a criminal offense in Germany and can be punished under §154 of the German Criminal Code with a prison sentence of six months to five years, the breach of an oath of office, such as that of the German chancellor, is not punishable.[13] As a rule, these oaths are not a prerequisite for assuming office but a consequence thereof.

For legal reasons alone, this understanding is central for a professional oath of teachers. It can only be the consequence of and not the prerequisite for assuming a school teaching position. Accordingly, a breach of the expressed obligations is above all a matter of conscience for the individual. This can certainly become a cause for discussion among all parties involved, but it is not linked to far-reaching sanctions. One exception should be emphasised at this point: human dignity, and with it the physical, mental, and spiritual integrity of the children entrusted to the teacher's care. If a teacher breaks with these principles, they have left the field of conscience, and legal steps should be initiated with all consequences under private, employment, and, if necessary, civil service law.

In educational discussions about a professional oath, reference is repeatedly made to the Hippocratic Oath, which makes sense insofar as the professions of a doctor and a teacher certainly have parallels. According to Ewald Terhart, in both of them 'administrative control and supervision from the outside is neither sensible nor possible due to the structural peculiarities of the work processes', and both 'are very strongly based on relational and emotional work'. In this sense, a professional oath compensates for the risk that 'a society takes by delegating the solution of serious, or at least perceived serious, social and/or individual problems to a certain occupational group and thereby tolerating the formation of a monopoly'.[14]

In contrast to the physician, who is essentially only obligated to care for the patient, teachers assume a double mandate, for they must fulfil the educational mandate entrusted to them by constitutional law vis-à-vis the student on the one hand and society on the other. Helmut Fend has elaborated this aspect within the framework of a theory of school.[15] 'A profession with such difficult tasks and such a wide scope of discretion in the choice of means to carry them out', concludes Wolfgang Brezinka, 'can only be fulfilled satisfactorily by someone who has a morally positive attitude towards the tasks of the profession and towards the norms that apply to its exercise, and who habitually experiences them as obligatory for I'.[16]

Since in the meantime these considerations have also been corroborated by a multitude of empirical results from professional research, teacher professionalism is seen as a symbiosis of competence and attitude with regard to the subject, pedagogy, and didactics. Successful teachers therefore not only have the necessary knowledge and skills but also bring with them a corresponding will and judgement.[17]

Notes

1 Cf. Hentig, H. (1991): Der neue Eid. In: *DIE ZEIT*, Nr. 39.

2 Hentig, H. v. (2016): *Noch immer mein Leben. Erinnerungen und Kommentare aus den Jahren 2005 bis 2015*. Berlin, p. 477f.

3 Habermas, J. (1989): Heidegger – Werk und Weltanschauung. In: Farias, V. (Hrsg.): *Heidegger und der Nationalsozialismus*. Frankfurt, p. 11–37; here p. 12. My translation.

4 Habermas (1989), l. c., p. 14. My translation.

5 Cf. Zierer, K. (2021a): Erhard Wiersing: Hartmut von Hentig – Ein Essay zu Leben und Werk. In: *Zeitschrift für Päda-gogik*, Heft 6, p. 972–976.

6 Cf. Hentig (1991), l. c.

7 The topic of a professional oath has been taken up in educational science again and again. These contributions range from conceptual reflections to empirical work. Cf. Giesecke, H. (1997): *Die pädagogische Beziehung*. Weinheim, p. 265f.; Terhart, E. (1987): Vermutungen über das Lehrerethos. In: *Zeitschrift für Pädagogik*, 6, p. 787–804; Drahmann, M. & Cramer, C. (2019): Vermutungen über das Lehrerethos – revisited. In: Cramer, C. & Oser, F.: *Ethos – Interdisziplinäre Perspektiven auf den Lehrerinnen- und Lehrerberuf*. Münster, p. 15–36; Brinkmann, M. & Rödel, S.S. (2021): Ethos im Lehrerberuf – Haltung zeigen und Haltung üben. In: *Journal für LehrerInnenbildung*, 3, p. 42–62; Rychner, M. (2015): Der sokratische Eid, professionstheoretisch gelesen. In: *Journal für LehrerInnenbildung*, 3, p. 42–46.

8 Cf. www.encyclopedia.com/history/dictionaries-thesauruses-pictures-and-press-releases/teachers-loyalty-oath (retrieved on 25.02.2023).

9 Cf. www.oaj.fi/en/education/ethical-principles-of-teaching/comenius-oath-for-teachers/ (retrieved on 24.02.2023).

10 Cf. www.teacherph.com/2016-oath-taking-professional-teachers/ (retrieved on 24.02.2023).

11 Cf. www.ndtv.com/education/teachers-day-kalams-10-oaths-for-teachers-1746387 (retrieved on 24.02.2023).

12 Cf. www.comp.nus.edu.sg/~tantc/personal/pledge.html und vgl. www.mekulipress.com/betimi-i-mesuesit/ (retrieved on 24.02.2023).

13 Cf. www.bundestag.de/resource/blob/585474/a98216050ea29dcda726f464caa1f236/WD-3-368-18-pdf-data.pdf (retrieved on 24.02.2023).

14 Terhart (1987), l. c., p. 788.

15 Fend, H. (2008): *Neue Theorie der Schule*. Wiesbaden.

16 Brezinka, W. (1986): *Erziehung in einer wertunsicheren Gesellschaft*. Munich, p. 181. My translation.

17 Cf. Hattie & Zierer (2020), l. c., p. 25.

3 What characterises teacher professionalism?

The introductory situation of this book, according to which we spend 15,000 hours in school in the course of our lives and are taught by about 50 teachers, often leads in reflection to the fact that we can remember four or five good teachers as well as seven or eight bad ones. The problem is not that there are good and bad teachers. The remarkable thing is that most of the teachers we once had disappear into thin air, whereas a handful manage to be remembered positively for a lifetime.

These are the teachers we are talking about. They were teachers who had a great influence on our learning and also on our education – and still do today. The focus will be on looking at what they did, how they did what they did, and why they did what they did. And the challenge of bringing these perspectives together leads to the question of what teacher professionalism is. Drawing on a variety of approaches, I will attempt in the following to provide a description of the construct 'teacher professionalism'.

In 2009, Simon Sinek, a US motivator and book author, gave a TED talk entitled 'How great leaders inspire action'. Within a very short time, this talk generated worldwide discussion and remains the third most viewed film on TED.com – nearly 60 million views in the last eight years. Shortly after the talk, Simon Sinek published the book *Start with Why*, in which he presents his thoughts in a more nuanced way:[1]

At first glance, his idea is perhaps too simple to be true: How are three concentric circles, provided with the words 'What?', 'How?', and 'Why?', supposed to explain success? Only at second glance do the interrelationships involved turn out to be helpful in describing successful personnel management. And those interrelationships can also be used to better understand pedagogical expertise.

Simon Sinek argues that successful action can be viewed from three different perspectives: First, it can be examined from the perspective of what is being done. Second, it can be examined from the perspective of asking how something is done can be taken. And third, it is possible to ask why something

DOI: 10.4324/9781003439288-3

is done. To illustrate his thoughts, Simon Sinek uses the following drawing, which he calls the Golden Circle:[2]

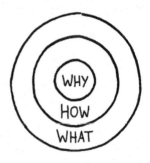

Simon Sinek's core message is that many people begin and also end their reflections with the outer circle. They ask about what they are doing and often do not think further. The far more important questions of how and why they do what they do are thus not asked at all. On this path, many people often lose sight of the original goal and thus also fail at their central task. The result is a meaningless, mechanical reaction to external stimuli and a failure to act from within. Successful action looks different. Here, the question of why something has to be done is at the centre of considerations. It leads to the question of how to do something and finally of what to do. Following Simon Sinek, the key point is therefore that successful action does not involve only deciding what to do. Much more important is how and why one does what one does. Consequently, the secret of success in his eyes is to start with the inner circle and the question of why and go outward from there to connect the questions of how and what.

To illustrate his thoughts, Simon Sinek presents three examples: Apple, Dr. Martin Luther King, Jr., and the Wright Brothers.

What is the secret of Apple's success? Certainly, it's not what Apple does: Apple makes computers, tablets, and cell phones – just like many other companies. And if you take a closer look at these devices, you have to admit that they're not that much better than the competition – a phone that bends in your pocket is a unique selling point but certainly not in a positive sense.[3] Likewise, it's not because of how Apple does what it does. Rather, a detailed examination from this perspective reveals just the opposite: low wages, high environmental impact, and poor working conditions. In this respect, the secret to Apple's success is to ask why: Anyone who buys an Apple today gets not only a technical device but also a philosophy of life, an attitude to life, a passion. Apple stands for the feeling of living a better life.

Why is Dr. Martin Luther King, Jr. the most famous and influential leader of the African American civil rights movement? Certainly not solely because of what he did. He was not the only humanist of the time, and his ideas were the ideas of a larger group of activists. Nor was it solely because of how he did what he did. Undoubtedly he was an outstanding speaker with fire and passion, but even that did not set him apart from his peers in any decisive way. Therefore, the reason for Martin Luther King's success must be sought elsewhere: Why did he do what he did? The 250,000 people who made their way to Washington on 28 August 1963 did not get an invitation. They came because they believed in Martin Luther King – not so much in what he said or how he said it but in why he said it. Martin Luther King had a vision of why he was doing what he was doing. 'I have a dream' are his immortal words – not 'I have a plan'. The people who heard Martin Luther King that day were deeply moved, shared the same values, and had a common vision. They all believed that this day would change everything.

On 17 December 1903, the Wright brothers became the first people to succeed in flying an engine-powered aeroplane. Why them of all people? Compared with other teams competing with them, they had the worst conditions: no sponsorship, no government support, no outstanding relations, and no special education. Compared with their most famous opponent, Samuel Pierpont Langley, they should have lost the race for the crown of aviation pioneers. After all, Langley was not only a professor at the United States Naval Academy; he also had the best contacts in government circles and sufficient funding. So why still the Wright brothers? Undoubtedly, both teams were highly motivated, had a clear goal in mind, and worked hard for success. The difference, however, was not luck or good fortune. It was inspiration: While the Langley team wanted to be the first to achieve fame and glory, the Wright brothers were about vision, faith, the dream of flying. The Langley team was motivated by what they were doing, while the Wright brothers were focused on the why of what they were doing.

Simon Sinek's core message is thus demonstrated by the success of Apple, Martin Luther King, and the Wright brothers: They all started not with the question of what they were doing but with the question of why they were doing what they were doing. They all had a vision, a passion, a belief, and they were able to communicate and share all of that with others.

It is surprising and fascinating that Simon Sinek's core message, gleaned from his experience and expertise, finds an empirical match: Howard Gardner, along with Mihály Csíkszentmihályi and William Damon, launched the Good Work Project in 1995.[4] In it, the three scholars sought to clarify the question: What characterises successful work? To answer this question, they conducted more than 1,200 interviews with people from nine different professions to understand how they define professional success and how good work can be recognised. From the extensive data set, they derived a supposedly simple formula: Good work is characterised by '3 Es': excellence, engagement, and ethics. A successful worker knows what they are doing, cares about it, and can give reasons for what they are doing. It is irrelevant whether we are talking about the work of a cleaner or the work of a top manager: Good work is a matter of excellence, engagement, and ethics.

To illustrate this idea, let's take an example from everyday life. Please imagine the following situation: You order a cup of coffee in a bar. In the first case, the waitress serves you the cup of coffee by communicating with you in a friendly and appreciative manner so that you feel that you are a welcome guest. In the second case, the waitress serves you the cup of coffee without talking to you, not even looking at you, making you feel unwelcome. In both cases, the cup of coffee is in front of you. So the result is the same, but still it is not the same, and these two cases illustrate the core message of the 3 Es: Good work is not only a matter of excellence, that is, the knowledge and skills needed to do the job, but also and above all of commitment, that is, the motivation regarding the job, and ethics, that is, the values and the reasons that are always associated with a job.

In short, it turns out that serving a cup of coffee can be of different quality even though the cup of coffee is always in front of us. The quality depends crucially on the excellence, engagement, and ethics of the service. In terms of the above discussion of Simon Sinek, excellence can be linked to what, engagement to how, and ethics to why. In this respect, it is possible to connect and illustrate Simon Sinek's considerations with the findings of Howard Gardner, Mihály Csíkszentmihályi, and William Damon. Once again, the circular model provides an apt illustration:

In the following, these considerations will be the basis for explaining pedagogical expertise. For this purpose, it is helpful to focus on what many consider to be the core of pedagogy in general and of teaching in particular: teacher subject matter knowledge.

It is one of the most persistent myths in the discussion of educational science that a successful teacher is one who possesses a particularly high level of teacher subject matter knowledge. The entire university teacher education system is based on this assumption and accordingly gives the greatest space to specialised studies. And whenever reforms in teacher education are discussed, the call for more teacher subject matter knowledge has a firm place.

But how can it be that teacher subject matter knowledge has almost no effect at all on student learning performance in empirical studies?[5]

The didactic triangle, an old, if not the oldest, model of pedagogy can help to understand these results. The protagonists of teaching – teacher, learners, and subject – serve as a basis for distinguishing between three dialogic structures: first, a dialogue between teacher and learners; second, a dialogue between learners and content; and third, a dialogue between teacher and content. Since these dialogues intertwine in practice, it follows that the didactic triangle should be an equilateral triangle. That is, the relationships and the interactions between teacher, learners, and content should be balanced and in equilibrium. It should be pointed out at this point that teaching is always embedded in a certain structure, so that a multitude of other aspects have an effect on it. For example, social, political, and cultural conditions should be considered with regard to the external structure, and situational conditions, such as the design of the classroom, the individual well-being of all those involved, time constraints, and so on, should be considered with regard to the internal structure. The following figure summarises this in a familiar way:

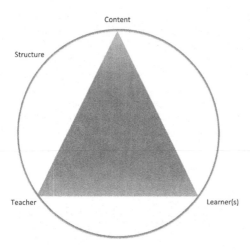

If one assumes that teaching only takes place when the three dialogic structures are recognisable, then an explanation can be found for the low effectiveness of teacher subject matter knowledge:[6] Teacher subject matter knowledge creates the dialogic structure between the teacher and the subject matter – no more, but also no less. In this respect, teaching cannot be held without subject matter competence or with it alone. It requires more.

We all know people who know an enormous amount but cannot explain it. They lack didactic competence, which is responsible for the dialogic structure between the learners and the content. For example, the teacher is faced with the challenge of designing the learning environment in such a way that it is possible for the learners to grasp the subject matter. An adequate selection of methods, such as teaching principles and forms of work and action, social forms, teaching forms, and learning forms, is just as much a part of this as an appropriate design of media, temporal and spatial structuring, and adjustment of the goals and content to fit the learning situation of the learners. However, the fact that didactic competence alone is just as insufficient as subject matter competence is shown, for example, by the factor 'teacher verbal ability', for which empirical studies also report a low effectiveness on learning performance.[7]

We also all know people who know an enormous amount but are so unapproachable that one would prefer not to be in the same room with them. These people cannot relate to other people, and they lack pedagogical competence, which is crucial for the dialogic structure between the learners and the teacher. For example, the teacher must be able to enter into a conversation with the learners, must be able to build an atmosphere of trust and confidence, and must provide security in the teaching–learning process. This is underpinned by the great effectiveness reported in empirical studies for the factor 'teacher–student relationships'.

In this respect, teacher subject matter knowledge alone is not enough to be able to teach successfully. It must be flanked by didactic and pedagogical competence, and only in this triad can it become effective. A corresponding interaction is therefore crucial. We need a high level of subject matter competence and an equally high level of didactic and pedagogical competence. For the sake of completeness, it should be mentioned that teachers must be able to analyse, understand, and take into account the internal and external framework conditions of teaching. They therefore need systemic competence. The following figure tries to clarify this:

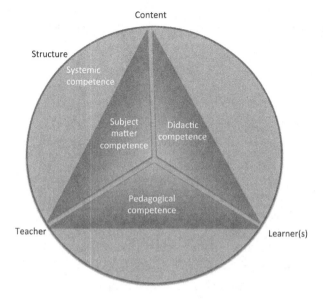

Consequently, subject matter competence, didactic competence, and pedagogical competence should not be seen as opposites but as parts of a greater whole. If we look at current teacher training against this background and how it is designed in many countries, we can see that there are definitely shortcomings: The first phase at the universities is dominated by subject matter competence while hardly addressing pedagogical and didactic competence, and the interconnectedness of these areas of competence is not addressed at all. The second phase, the first years of professional life, is dominated by pedagogical and didactic competence while at the same time relying on the subject matter competence acquired at university, and here, too, there is hardly any networking. In the third phase, that is, until retirement, things become 'autodidactic': Everyone is the architect of their own fortune, and teacher training culminates in – or degenerates into – boundless freedom. Professional teacher training should look different.

As convincing as this argumentation may be, the triad of subject matter competence, didactic competence, and pedagogical competence is not sufficient for successful teaching. In fact, we have known for a long time that in pedagogical contexts, it is important not only what we do but also and above all how and why we do something. In this respect, it is not only competence in the form of knowledge and skills that is crucial but above all attitude in the form of will and values, and the latter determines whether the former is brought into play. Once again, this idea may be illustrated with the help of the didactic triangle:

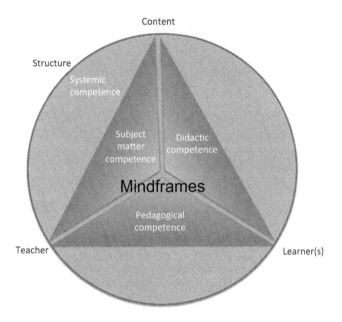

The example of mistakes can be used to illustrate this: A teacher can know everything about mistakes and also know procedures that help learners to learn from mistakes. But what if this teacher believes that mistakes are something to be avoided? And what if this teacher does not examine the mistakes that the learners make every day or the ones he makes himself because he does not consider them important? And what if this teacher tells the learners that mistakes are best avoided? The result will be an atmosphere of fear, where learners are afraid to make a mistake. This diminishes creativity, courage, and even joy. How different is the situation for a teacher who also has the knowledge and skills to use mistakes for constructive criticism in the classroom but has developed a positive attitude toward mistakes because she considers them important in the educational process? This teacher will look for errors in order to know where learners stand, what they can already do, and what they cannot yet do. This teacher will pick up on mistakes and then provide assistance accordingly. And the learners will not be afraid of mistakes but will recognise that mistakes are part of learning and are important because they make it clear what has already been mastered and what needs to be looked at more closely.

It is obvious how this is connected to the arguments of Simon Sinek, as well as those of Howard Gardner, Mihály Csíkszentmihályi, and William Damon: Successful action in school and teaching requires not only knowledge and ability (understood as excellence and the question of what), but also will (understood as commitment and the question of how) and values (understood as ethics and the question of why). What is particularly interesting here is the observation that there is an internal connection between these aspects: Ability is based on knowledge, which is only retrieved when there is a will. And as there are always reasons for this, willingness is based on a value. Against this background, pedagogical action shows itself to be a profoundly ethical action. If, for example, a teacher can draw on the necessary ability, knowledge, will, and values, they will act accordingly in a situation, and if the context is favourable, they will be successful in their actions. If one of the mentioned aspects is missing, for example the will, the teacher will most likely fail in their actions. The following figure summarises this argumentation and develops the ACAC model (attitude, competence, action, context):

It is obvious that a high level of competence alone does not establish expertise, just as the best attitudes are not sufficient for this. Instead, it is the interplay between competence and attitude that counts. If one looks at the biography of a teacher against this background, it can be seen that it is above all attitude that is at stake throughout a lifetime: While knowledge and ability in the field of school and teaching are manageable, will and values are put to the test day in and day out. And ultimately, it is attitudes that determine whether one will successfully pursue the challenging profession of teaching throughout one's life.

It is also clear that promoting competence is an easy task compared with changing one's attitudes. But should we shy away from it because of that? If we want to develop pedagogical expertise, we have no choice but to accept this challenge and place it at the centre of teacher education.

Successful teachers have a passion not only for the subject but also for didactics and pedagogy, for learners, and for their profession. And this passion is not only important to becoming a successful teacher. It is also important in order to pursue this challenging profession throughout one's life, that is, to remain a successful teacher.

Against the background of these considerations and in view of the extensive data provided by empirical educational research, John Hattie and I speak of 'mindframes'.[8] By this we mean the symbiosis of competence and attitudes. It is what makes successful teachers stand out. In an attempt to summarise the vast body of research on effective teaching and learning, I would like to formulate the following ten mindframes:

1) I am an evaluator of my impact on student learning.

I am very good at making my impact on student learning visible. I know that student achievements make my impact visible and help me to maximise my impact. My goal is to evaluate my impact on student learning regularly and systematically, and I need to use student learning to assess my impact.

2) I see assessment as informing my impact and next steps.

I am very good at adapting my teaching when my students do not achieve their learning goals and at using the achievement of my students to draw conclusions about my thoughts concerning goals, content, methods, and media. My goal is to measure the achievement levels of my students regularly and systematically and use objective methods of measuring student achievement to assess the success of my teaching.

3) I collaborate with my peers and my students about my conceptions of progress and my impact.

I am very good at saving time by sharing work with other teachers and sharing responsibility on teams. I know perfectly well that failures can be overcome on a team and that responsibility can be shared in a team. My goal is always to consolidate strengths through teamwork and overcome failures in my team. I am thoroughly convinced that it is important to cooperate with my colleagues.

4) I am a change agent and believe that all students can improve.

I am very good at applying successful methods to make my teaching more differentiated and applying various strategies for enhancing students' motivation. My goal is always to have an impact on the students through my teaching and to motivate them in their learning process. I am thoroughly convinced that I have a positive impact on students and that it is important to continuously question the impact of my teaching.

5) I strive for challenges and not merely to 'do my best'.

I am very good at developing challenging assignments based on learning levels and setting challenging learning goals appropriate to the students' learning needs. I know that the assignments in my lessons and the learning requirements should be challenging. My goal is always to design my lesson to include challenging goals for the students based on their learning level. I am thoroughly convinced that it is important for students to make an effort and that suitable challenging goals can be formulated only on the basis of the learning level.

6) I give and help students understand feedback, and I interpret and act on feedback given to me.

I am very good at obtaining feedback from my students and using it to improve my teaching. I know that I need to act on feedback from my students, and I know how to give and help students understand feedback. My goal is always to obtain feedback from my students and reflect on it. I am thoroughly convinced that regular feedback strategies need to be integrated into my lessons and that I should use my students' opinions as feedback.

7) I engage as much in dialogue as in monologue.

I am very good at encouraging students to talk about content and leading them to learning success through cooperation with others. I know that instructions need to be clearly formulated, and I am aware of the benefits of cooperative learning methods, such as the think–pair–share strategy. My goal is always to encourage students to communicate more with each other and present their thinking and solution processes more often. I am thoroughly convinced that students should communicate with each other and that it is important to get students to participate often in class.

8) I explicitly inform students about what successful impact looks like from the outset.

I am very good at showing the learner what the goal of the lesson is and what the criteria for successful learning are. I know that learning needs clear, challenging, and transparent goals and that the visibility of the criteria for success is an essential aid for learners. My goal is always to make the objectives of teaching clear, challenging, and transparent and to show learners the criteria for success.

9) I build relationships and trust so that learning can occur in a place where it is safe to make mistakes and learn from others.

I am very good at taking into account my students' environment and establishing a feeling of belonging in the class. I know that a positive relationship with students is important and that the students' environment has great influence on their learning. My goal is always to get my students to trust me and to build trust among my students. I am thoroughly convinced that a positive relationship with my students is important and that it is important to establish a fair and positive climate in the class.

10) I focus on learning and the language of learning.

I am very good at identifying the strengths and weaknesses of my students and determining what prior academic knowledge my students have. I know that my students' prior experiences need to be taken into account and what achievement level my students are at. My goal is always to take into account the strengths, weaknesses, and prior academic knowledge of my students. I focus on learning and the language of learning when teaching.

Notes

1 Cf. Sinek, S. (2009): *Start with Why – How Great Leaders Inspire Everyone to Take Action*. New York.
2 Cf. Sinek (2009), l. c.
3 Cf. www.derwesten.de/wirtschaft/nutzer-klagen-iphone-6-plus-verbiegt-sich-in-hosentasche-id9861181.html (retrieved on 25.02.2023).
4 Cf. Gardner, H., Csíkszentmihályi, M. & Damon, W. (2005): *Good Work*. Stuttgart.
5 Cf. Hattie & Zierer (2020), l. c., p. 24, and Baumert, J. & Kunter, M. (2006): Stichwort: Professionelle Kompetenz von Lehrkräften. In: *Zeitschrift für Erziehungswissenschaft*, 9, p. 469–452; Blömeke, S., Kaiser, G. & Lehmann, R. (Eds.) (2010):

TEDS-M 2008: Professionelle Kompetenz und Lerngelegenhei-ten angehender Primarstufenlehrkräfte im internationalen Vergleich. Münster; Kunter, M., Baumert, J., Blum, W., Klusmann, U., Krauss, S. & Neubrand, M. (Eds.) (2011): *Professionelle Kompetenz von Lehrkräften. Ergebnisse des Forschungsprogramms COACTIV.* Münster, und Pant, H.A., Stanat, P., Schroeders, U., Roppelt, A., Siegle, T. & Pöhlmann, C. (2013): *IQB-Ländervergleich 2012.* Münster.

6 Cf. Zierer, K. (2015): Educational Expertise: The Concept of 'Mind Frames' as an Integrative Model for Professionalisation in Teaching. In: *Oxford Review of Education,* 41(6), p. 782–798, http://dx.doi.org/10.1080/03054985.2015.1121140 (retrieved on 24.02.2023).

7 Cf. Hattie, J. (2013): *Visible Learning for Teachers.* London.

8 Cf. Hattie, J. & Zierer, K. (2018): *10 Mindframes for Visible Learning.* London.

4 What can be understood by 'attitudes', and why are they crucial for a professional oath?

At this point in the discourse, a debate often ignites: Does a corresponding understanding of the profession mean an ethic of attitudes? Are attitudes not something that cannot be learned at all? Should a professional oath lead to a standardisation of thinking and acting? Certainly these positions also exist in educational science; for example, Wolfgang Brezinka calls for a teaching of attitudes in teacher training.[1] It can be demonstrated through the aforementioned concept of attitudes that this conclusion has to be considered with caution.[2]

Attitudes are currently experiencing a renaissance. One encounters them in election and advertising posters across parties and camps: in attitudes against the right, in asylum policy, against agitation, in animal welfare, and so on. Attitudes play a role in almost all social issues. This must come as a surprise in view of the not only positive but also problematic history of the concept of attitudes. After all, attitudes were at the centre of a Posen speech by the German National Socialist Heinrich Himmler at a point when it was about the attitude of the SS man.

Against this background, conceptual reflection seems indispensable. In line with the classical procedure of the term explication, the following interpretation will take into account etymological and everyday language aspects as well as scientific findings.

The word 'attitude' comes from the Italian word 'attitudine', which itself goes back to the Latin word 'aptitudo', translated as 'aptitude' or 'ability'. This Latin word derives from the verb 'aptus', which means 'to fit' or 'to join'. Two meanings of 'attitude' have emerged over time: first, the (appropriate) posture of the body and second, a mental attitude or approach to a situation.

For the concept of attitude as discussed in the context of a professional oath, the second meaning is of interest. It becomes apparent that attitudes are observable from the outside, that is, from other people, but can at the same time be observed from within and consequently from each individual person. The latter presupposes a self-awareness that is essential in the scientific analysis of the concept of attitude.

If one looks at the history of the concept against this background, it reaches back to antiquity. For example, in Aristotle's *Nicomachean Ethics* we find the

DOI: 10.4324/9781003439288-4

word 'hexis', which is central to virtue ethics:[3] It is true that humans cannot do anything about the circumstances that befall them and the resulting feelings. But they are responsible for how they live with these circumstances and what they make of them. A related understanding of self and world represents a concretisation of the general determination of attitudes as relating to self and world. The implied characteristic of stability is further elaborated by Otto Friedrich Bollnow when he contrasts attitudes with moods:[4] While moods are something that can change quickly and are in that regard volatile, attitudes turn out to be constant and enduring without being unchangeable or rigid. Unlike moods, attitudes change as the result of profound experiences, again addressing self-consciousness as a category.

Another dichotomy becomes visible depending on whether the concept of attitude is used in the singular or in the plural. On the one hand, a person can develop a basic attitude toward life as a whole, but on the other hand, this attitude consists of a number of partial attitudes toward individual questions of life. The latter is the basis for a professional attitude that should be demanded in the context of education and teaching.

If these aspects of the concept of attitude appear to be more or less free of contradictions, the difficulties reveal themselves when one looks at the current international discourse. There is a confusion of terms, including attitudes, values, convictions, beliefs, habitus, efficacy, mindset, and mindframes, to name just a few. What is what and how is one related to the other? These questions cannot be answered conclusively in the following, but an attempt at order will be presented nevertheless:

Ken Wilber developed an integral epistemology on the basis of the main approaches of Eastern and Western philosophy.[5] Its main message is that complex phenomena may be observed from different perspectives and that each and every one of these perspectives is important on its own. He accordingly regards it as problematic to argue from a single perspective. What Ken Wilber thus does is essentially to differentiate between four approaches to knowledge that open up different facets with regard to attitudes:

subjective	*objective*
Intentional	Behavioral
intersubjective	*interobjective*
Cultural	Social (Systems)

The first is an objective approach to the self and the world the basis of which is empirical data. It achieves a gain in knowledge by means of measurements, tests, and the like. An example of a statement in this quadrant might be 'It's raining outside'. This statement can be verified quickly and easily by anyone. It is therefore clear that statements taking the objective approach make truth claims. This approach is currently the dominant one in nearly all societal and scientific domains. When we speak of knowledge today, what we generally mean is knowledge that may be classified as belonging to this quadrant. From a conceptual standpoint, attitudes here become objective, as reflected in statements like 'On the basis of empirical studies, I am of the opinion that the reduction of class sizes can only be effective if teachers change their teaching'. Attitudes have to be measurable, and only if they are measurable are they objective positions.

The second is a subjective approach to the self and the world. This approach is primarily about needs, interests, and feelings. An example would be 'I'm fine' as a response to the question 'How are you?' The truth content of this statement clearly defies verification by empirical means: It is not possible to verify through measurements and tests whether the person providing response is telling the truth or lying. We can try to gain additional information by studying the person's facial expression and gestures, but ultimately we are forced to remain at the level of interpretation: We can interpret and attempt to understand how much truth there is in such a statement, but we can never be absolutely certain that our interpretation is correct. Ken Wilber hence posits that statements belonging to the subjective quadrants make claims not to truth but to truthfulness. These arguments are also particularly true of human will; it too defies measurement and testing but is crucial for thought and action. Attitudes appear in the shape of desires, needs, and interests motivated primarily from a first-person perspective. They are, hence, 'my' desires, 'my' needs, and 'my' interests. The validity claim connected with these forms of will and judgement is limited to the individual and cannot simply be applied unchanged to other people. This also includes expressions of belief, as already confirmed by the statement 'I believe' on its own. From a conceptual standpoint, attitudes therefore become subjective beliefs, as articulated in statements like 'I think that you love me'.

The third is an intersubjective approach to the self and the world. Its key elements are the values, norms, rules, and rituals that influence how people think and act. They can neither be defined empirically nor prescribed by an individual. Rather, they need to be examined in an argumentative and discursive process if they are to attain general acceptance in society. In this respect, statements from the intersubjective approach do not make a claim to truth or to truthfulness but rather to what Ken Wilber terms cultural fit. As an illustration, consider what values a person's thoughts and actions are determined by and where these values come from. It is not the individual alone who decides what is important and what is not, what is culturally appropriate and what is not; rather, the individual is influenced greatly in their values by the collective, which may be illustrated by the influence of family in the first years of human life. The collective agrees upon these values, norms, rules, and rituals in a process of exchange and discourse, and these are then valid not just for the individual but for all people who regard themselves as belonging to this group. From a conceptual standpoint, attitudes therefore become collective judgements in this case, as articulated in statements like 'We believe that human dignity is inviolable'.

And finally, the fourth approach to knowledge is an interobjective approach to the self and the world, the basis of which are the systemic contexts that become visible in role assignments. No person exists for themself alone but is integrated into various contexts – into family, into an economic and political system, and into a church, to name what are perhaps the most important ones. According to the systems theory of Niklas Luhmann, which can be associated with this approach, there are numerous points of tension between the individual systems. They may be attributed above all to the different codes with which these systems communicate and work: Politics is primarily a matter of power, economy a matter of profit, church a matter of faith, and so on. These varying interests can spark conflicts and controversies, and the individual is called upon to overcome these tensions by means of thought and action. It is above all ability that determines whether the individual is capable of forming the different role expectations into a coherent whole. It is therefore a matter of achieving a functional fit, as Ken Wilber terms it. Attitudes here are systemic positions. Their claim to validity is detached from the individual, as well as from the group. On the basis of empirical results, they try to take a systemic position, as in the statement 'In light of many studies, I believe that early language support not only relieves the burden on the family but helps society as a whole'.

Against the backdrop of this argumentation, the concept of attitude takes on a more differentiated meaning: Attitudes can – depending on what experiences they appeal to – become beliefs and judgements. If attitudes are based on a subjective context, they are essentially subjective beliefs. If, on the other hand, they are based on an intersubjective context, they may be described primarily as collective judgements. And if they are based on an objective or interobjective context, they take on the form of objective or systemic positions.

In this respect, attitudes always comprise subjective beliefs, collective judgements, objective positions, and interobjective positions. Since there can be contradictions between these facets – a person can be a passionate hunter but also an advocate of animal welfare – the characteristic of attitudes is not that they are consistent but that they are coherent. This coherence again points to the changeability of attitudes. After all, inconsistency can lead to self-consciousness. The following figure summarises this argumentation for pedagogical attitudes:[6]

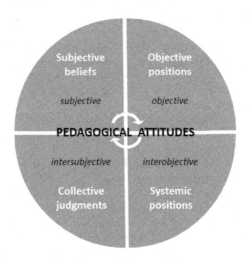

These considerations show that the concept of attitude is suitable for eliminating a historical split between humanities education on the one hand and empirical educational research on the other. These camps have existed for decades, and they are 'particularly fatal' in the context of a professional oath. As Ewald Terhart concludes:

While the empirical research programme describes processes, the other discussion context elaborates systems of norms and catalogues of virtues as well as their respective systematic justifications. However, as long as one only elaborates how things should be, and the other only proves again and again that this is not how things are, no mutual learning, no systematic progress in knowledge is possible.[7]

Attitudes find themselves precisely in this mediating role because they encompass subjective beliefs, collective judgements, systemic positions, and objective positions and form them into a coherent whole. Against this background, what describes the professional biographical task is not being a teacher as a result of having become a teacher but remaining a teacher.

It is precisely this space of possibility that becomes evident in the context of professionalisation. That is, it is not a matter of a one-sided ethics of attitude (according to the principle 'The main thing is to have the right attitudes!') or an ethics of responsibility (according to the principle 'The main thing is to achieve the goal!'). Rather, following Max Weber,[8] it must be about a professional ethics that asks about the causes as well as the consequences of action in the light of humanity and a resulting understanding of education.

Notes

1 Cf. Brezinka (1986), l. c.
2 Cf. Zierer, K. (2020): Stichwort Haltungen. In: *weiter bilden*, 3, p. 10–11.
3 Cf. Aristoteles (1956): *Nikomachische Ethik*. Berlin.
4 Cf. Bollnow, O.F. (2009): *Das Wesen der Stimmungen*. Würzburg.
5 Cf. Wilber, K. (2002): *Eros, Kosmos, Logos – Eine Jahrtausend-Vision*. Frankfurt, and Habermas, J. (1995): *Theorie des kommunikativen Handelns*. Frankfurt.
6 Cf. Zierer, K., Lachner, C., Tögel, J. & Weckend, D. (2018): Teacher Mindframes from an Educational Science Perspective. In: *Education Sciences*, 8(4), p. 209, https://doi.org/10.3390/educsci8040209
7 Terhart (1987), l. c., p. 794.
8 Cf. Weber, M. (1992): *Politik als Beruf*. Stuttgart.

5   Why is Socrates suitable as a guarantor for a professional oath for teachers?

It may come as a surprise that Hartmut von Hentig, when he first published the Socratic Oath in 1991, did not give any reasons for choosing Socrates as the guarantor of his reflections.[1] A look at his biography gives an idea of why: As an ancient coin philologist, Hartmut von Hentig knew Greek antiquity in detail, and after almost thirty years as a professor in Göttingen (Germany), it was apparently more than natural for him to choose Socrates.[2]

This assessment is certainly no longer true today. Knowledge of Greek antiquity can no longer be taken for granted – certainly not in the discourse of educational science, which has developed in a different direction after several empirical turns. For this reason, it is necessary at this point to reveal Socrates's determination as a guarantor of a professional oath for teachers. So why Socrates of all people?

In the history of philosophy, Socrates stands for a turning point. 'With him', writes Günter Figal, 'begins what has since been called philosophy . . . with Socrates everything that existed before enters into a new light'.[3] Socrates was born in Alopeke in 469 BC and died in Athens in 399 BC after being tried for impiety and sentenced to death at the trial. He was made to drink a cup of hemlock, a common method of execution at the time. This event, like Socrates's entire philosophy, was not handed down by Socrates himself but by his students, first and foremost Platon.

The newness of Socrates's philosophy is best shown in Platon's dialogue *Sophist*. This dialogue does not talk about Socrates but about the important thinkers before his time, including Parmenides, Heraclitus, and Empedocles. It relates how these thinkers treated their listeners like children and 'told stories, unconcerned about whether you could follow them'.[4] With Socrates, this way of philosophising changed radically: He works with conversations, unfolds questions and answers, checks whether the interlocutor can follow or not. So while the pre-Socratics proclaimed their thoughts, Socrates is concerned with discussing his thoughts and unfolding them in dialogue. 'Through Socrates, thinking became conversation',[5] writes Günter Figal of this state of affairs. With this turn in the manner of exchange, Socrates shows himself to be a teacher, for his conversations always begin and end with his counterpart.

DOI: 10.4324/9781003439288-5

He does not want to instruct people but to help them develop their personality. We must, writes Hans Joachim Störig, imagine Socrates as a man-builder, 'driven by faith in humans and love for them . . . not as a teacher of general propositions'.[6]

The principles of his way of conducting conversations have become known under the term 'maieutics', which can be translated as 'midwifery'. To this day, it is disputed how realistic these 'ideal portraits' of Socrates and his approach that can be read in Platon and others are. Apart from this, the following principles are noteworthy from a pedagogical point of view: engagement with the learners, dialogical understanding, the closeness to life of the questions, trust in the learners' possibilities and confidence in their ability, avoidance of fear, consideration of prior knowledge and experience, authenticity of the teacher, the promotion of independence with the knowledge of the associated need for help, the appreciative treatment of the learners, the step-by-step approach, conscious practice and reflective consolidation, the consideration of the whole person in the unity of body-soul-spirit, the obtaining and giving of feedback, and much more.[7]

More important for the present book than the points mentioned above is the tradition that Socrates lived his life accordingly and did not compromise even in his defence speeches:

> If, therefore, as I have said, you would release me on this condition, I would say to you, I am indeed devoted to you and a friend, but I will obey the God more than you, and as long as I still breathe and am able, I will not cease to seek wisdom and to admonish and prove to you whomsoever of you I meet, with my usual speeches.[8]

The fact that Socrates accepts his death sentence so unreservedly is an expression of a piety which, in Günter Figal's view, is the basis for understanding Socrates's life and philosophy:

> It is better to die than to preserve one's life by acting shamefully . . . and, moreover, death is not a bad thing, because it is in any case the absence of the evils that beset life, and possibly even a better life.[9]

In other words, even at the hour of death, Socrates holds fast to his principles of life and remains true to his life and his philosophy.

'How could such a man, who was indeed a personality of moral greatness and died for his convictions, but whose actual philosophy is hardly tangible, have an immeasurable historical impact?' asks Hans Joachim Störig, and he gives the following answer: Socrates's influence is

> actually based more on his unique personality, which can still be close to us as human beings over the millennia, than on what he taught, namely in

that with him something entered the history of humanity which from then on became an ever more effective cultural force: the autonomous moral personality unshakably founded in itself.

This is the 'Socratic gospel' of the inwardly free human who does good for his or her own sake.[10]

Therefore, taking Socrates as a guarantor makes sense then and now. Socrates is a 'primus inter pares'. He can be regarded as one of the first teachers who had fundamental insights into education which can no doubt claim to be valid today. He implemented these principles in his dialogues and remained committed to them without any doubt throughout his life.

Notes

1 Against this background, it is important to distinguish that we are dealing with a 'Socratic Oath' and not with the 'Oath of Socrates'. The latter would mean that Socrates had spoken one and that it had been handed down.
2 Cf. to the biogrophy of Hartmut von Hentig Wiersing, E. (2020): *Hartmut von Hentig*. Bielefeld.
3 Figal, G. (2001): Sokrates. In: *Große Philosophen*. Darmstadt, p. 49–61, here S. 49. My translation.
4 Figal (2001), l. c., p. 49.
5 Figal (2001), l. c., p. 50.
6 Störig, H.J. (1998): *Kleine Weltgeschichte der Philosophie*. Frankfurt, p. 153. My translation.
7 Cf. Lütjen, J. (2013): *Das Bildungswegmodell zur Rehabilitation der sokratischen Mäeutik*. Hamburg, p. 421–430.
8 Platon (1892): *The Apology of Socrates*, 29D. Oxford.
9 Figal (2001), l. c., p. 52.
10 Störig (1998), l. c., p. 154.

6 Why is a renewal of the Socratic Oath necessary?

The mere reference to Hartmut von Hentig's involvement in the crimes committed at the Odenwald School is a sufficient reason for many to reject his Socratic Oath and demand a corresponding renewal. However, there are other valid reasons:

> It is part of the professional identity of doctors that there is a permanent and constant discussion about the Hippocratic Oath. New developments make it necessary to look at it again and again. But why should we think about a professional oath for teachers again today? What developments make a renewal of the Socratic Oath necessary? Is the welfare of children in such a bad state?[1]

'O tempora, o mores', is a quote by Cicero that pointedly describes a characteristic of we humans: We tend to see the world as being worse than it is. That's why it is above all negative headlines that can be sold. And the more of these negative headlines we hear and read, the more negative our image of the world becomes. But the image of the world thus gained does not necessarily correspond to the truth.

Against this backdrop, it is not surprising that two books adopting opposite positions have become bestsellers in recent years because in essence, both books are somewhat out of the ordinary, and in this sense 'negative' news. This is how they attract attention. The books are Hans Rosling's *Factfulness* and Steven Pinker's *Enlightenment Now*.[2] The core concern of both authors is to counteract the increasing populism and myth-making in the public debate – and to do so with facts and scientific findings. In a time marked by profound upheavals and a resulting uncertainty among many people, Hans Rosling and Steven Pinker see the answer in reflecting on what we really know. The quintessence of their argumentation is then also a different: We humans have never been as well off as we are today.

DOI: 10.4324/9781003439288-6

Hans Rosling and Steven Pinker derive this conclusion from their collection of data on almost all areas that are important to us humans. A foray will serve to clarify this in the following:

- Health: Globally, people are getting older and older. Average life expectancy is rising all over the world. This is partly due to advances in medical care. This is particularly evident in maternal and infant mortality, which are fortunately at a record low.
- Prosperity: Globally, the minimum income of people has never been as high as it is today. Consequently, fewer people than ever are affected by poverty.
- Peace: Globally, there have never been as many democracies as there are today. The democratisation process is advancing worldwide and consequently benefits all people.
- Education: Globally, the literacy rate has never been as high as it is today. Women in particular benefit from this development, as they are now able to receive schooling in more countries than ever before. This also means that the gender issue is a significant step further than it was decades ago.
- Environment: Globally, there have never been as many nature reserves as there are today. In terms of societies as a whole, environmental protection has arrived and is being promoted at various points. Even carbon emissions are being reduced: The progress that has been made in recent years points in the right direction. The air is getting better.

These figures are undoubtedly convincing, and they demonstrate emphatically that we humans have many possibilities. We humans are capable of solving many of the problems of our time through judgement and action. We humans can make the world a better place.

Nevertheless, I would like to pause at this point and present further developments that must make us sit up and take notice. Let's take a look at the previously mentioned areas once again:

- Health: It is true that the average life expectancy has never been as high as it is today. But it is also true that never before have so many people died from diseases of civilisation as today. As a result, people are getting older thanks to medical progress, but they are also becoming seriously ill earlier. The living environment that has been changed by people in the last decades is leading earlier and earlier to serious illnesses. Medical progress helps to prolong a life of illness.
- Prosperity: It is true that the average minimum income has risen steadily. But it is also true that the distribution of wealth has never been as disparate as it is today. In 2016, eight people alone owned 50 per cent of the world's wealth.

- Peace: It is true that the democratisation process is advancing globally. But it is also true that never before have so many people been on the run as today, because of war, torture, and displacement – according to current estimates, over 70 million people worldwide. And it is also true that in more and more countries, there is a right-wing camp gaining in importance that is concerned not with the one world but with the one nation state.
- Education: It is true that, globally speaking, education is accessible to more and more people. But it is also true that the average intelligence quotient has already passed its peak, and one can conclude that humanity is becoming dumber.
- Environment: It is true that there have never been as many nature reserves as there are today. But it is also true that the list of endangered animal and plant species has never been as long and the carpet of plastic waste in the world's oceans has never been as large as it is today.

This game – good numbers on the one side, bad numbers on the other side – could be played for longer. But this brief foray should suffice to conclude that it seems reductionist to say that the world is in balance and that we humans have never been as well off as we are today. For reality also includes the fact that the world is out of joint. We are facing challenges for society as a whole that we have never faced before. It would be naive to believe that the associated problems will somehow be solved. More than ever, judgement and action are required. Not because of the butterflies, the bees, or the birds but above all for our own sake. Nature will outlive humanity. But we run the risk of depriving ourselves of our livelihood.

Consequently, we humans are facing global challenges today. These include problems that we humans have caused and that can only be tackled by thinking globally. Following Wolfgang Klafki, we can speak of epochal challenges.[3] What is characteristic about these kinds of problems?

- They are of global significance and thus require global solutions. No nation state can cope with epochal challenges on its own.
- They have grown historically and come to the fore at a certain time. No nation state can avoid epochal challenges.
- They have an interdisciplinary character and cannot be viewed from only one perspective. Epochal challenges have at least one economic, one ecological, and one social facet.
- They require not only a factual analysis but also an ethical one. Consequently, different methodological approaches are needed to solve epochal challenges.

With this analysis, the crucial question is formulated: What should we do? This is the third of Kant's questions (What can I believe? What may I hope?

What should I do? Who is man?), and it has a pedagogical core, for it is not only a matter of describing the world as it is but also of helping to shape the world.

Recent developments have been marked by a number of such epochal challenges: the COVID-19 pandemic, the climate crisis, and the war in Ukraine, to name perhaps the most important ones. They are doubtlessly not inconsequential for the education of children and youth.

The measures taken to contain the COVID-19 pandemic, to elaborate on just one example, have primarily affected the well-being of children.[4] Whether it is cognitive learning performance, psychosocial development, or physical condition – in all these areas of personality development, it must be acknowledged in view of empirical data that the educational level is declining. In view of the correlation between level of education and a country's economic power,[5] this fact must already make us sit up and take notice, but it becomes even more striking in view of the correlation between level of education and a country's capacity for democracy.[6] For here, too, the following applies: If the one declines, so does the other. It is particularly dramatic that children from educationally disadvantaged backgrounds are more affected than children from educationally advantaged backgrounds, which can have an additional destabilising effect. Educational injustice is thus increasing because the education system is exacerbating existing educational inequalities instead of compensating for them.[7]

These developments alone would justify initiating a renewal of the Socratic Oath to give children a voice and bring their welfare to the centre of social discourse. There is no doubt that much was talked about in the COVID-19 pandemic, but relatively little was said about the welfare of children – and even less with the children themselves. Against this backdrop, it seems disconcerting that public educators, of all people, kept speaking out and calling for the most painful measure to contain the infections that can affect children: school closures.

In the light of empirical research, the digitalisation of education, which has been called for again and again in recent months and continues to be called for today, turns out to be less a saviour than a problem:[8] As important as digitalisation is and as decisive as it is for today's world, all that glitters is not gold. Digitalisation harbours a number of dangers and risks. Mobile phone addiction and cyber-bullying are just two phenomena that require pedagogical self-assurance and thus a renewal of the Socratic Oath because digitalisation for digitalisation's sake and thus without a pedagogical impetus runs the risk of becoming inhumane at schools but also in society as a whole.[9]

Without doubt, digital media enable new forms of communication and interaction by shifting the boundaries of space and time. Martin Heidegger understands space and time as *existentiell*:[10] From an ontological point of view, they are boundaries of humanness. Humans are always bound to a certain time and a certain space. They can escape neither their here nor their now.

Even if we manage to escape in our thoughts, we always return to our here and now. Digitalisation influences this here and now in a special way because it changes both not naturally but technically. Today we can communicate and interact with people all over the world at the same time with the help of digital media. Digital contacts are possible in a way that would never be possible in analogue form. At the same time, however, this increase in social contacts also increases the burden on us[11] because we have neither the time nor the space to deal with our social contacts at all times and in all places. So we reach our limits, and if we don't realise this, there is a risk of health problems. When too many messages reach us and demand an answer, it leads to psychological stress and subsequently to physical strain. This may include neck problems or even neuroplastic deformities, and the game Pokémon Go has even caused people to run to their death. This shows that the dissolution of the boundaries of space and time through digitalisation also leads to a dissolution of human boundaries.

Critics of technology have always pointed out that this dissolution of human boundaries is not without consequences, although it should be emphasised that critical does not mean destructive in the apocalyptic sense but rather discriminating and separating on the basis of reason and empiricism.[12] For example, Martin Heidegger already brings up this dissolution of human boundaries in his essay 'Die Frage nach der Technik' (The question concerning technology), without being able to have even an inkling at the time of what technology can make possible today. In his search for the essence of technology, he comes to the conclusion that technology can take away human freedom.[13] How is this to be understood? In *Die Antiquiertheit des Menschen* (The obsolescence of humankind), Günther Anders provides an answer to this question:[14] First, he defines humans as the limit of themselves. We humans have many possibilities, but at the same time, these possibilities are also our limits. Thus, we are certainly free beings, free from certain constraints and thus also free to decide. But this freedom is not limitless but is bound by the limits of human reason. With the help of technology, we are now able to shift our own limits. For example, we can increase and enhance our naturally limited computing power on demand through computer assistance: Computing operations that took several weeks in the pre-digital age can now be performed in seconds. Once this technology is in the world, it leads to human dependence and deprives us of our freedom.

The currently discussed chatbots make this problem particularly clear: They once again push the boundaries of humanness and thus also make us dependent, especially on space and time. As a result, it is not only human freedom that is at stake but also human reason because many people will blindly trust what the computer gives them as an answer to the questions asked. As is always the case with technical developments, it is not surprising that these effects are more pronounced among people from less educated backgrounds.

Technology in general and digitalisation as a technical manifestation in particular enable people to shift their boundaries. They lead to a dissolution of human boundaries. Günther Anders calls this shift a 'Promethean gap': The distance between humans and the world of products they have created is becoming ever greater. He draws three conclusions from this: 'that we are not equal to the perfection of our products; that we produce more than we can imagine and be responsible for; and that we believe that what we can do, we are also allowed to do, no: should, no: have to do'.[15]

The dissolution of human boundaries through digitalisation therefore calls in a special way for a reflection on the pedagogical leitmotif of humanism. Digitalisation is not an alternative to humanistically guided pedagogical practice but demands its continuation, even its radicalisation. The focus must be on the human being, our power of judgement, our strength of decision, and our thirst for action. Digital education must also be directed towards creating the conditions for us to be the authors of our own lives. In our view, 'humane education' in the age of digital transformation can, indeed must, be the guiding cultural idea.[16]

It may be acceptable that this digitalisation also costs a lot of money and creates a sustainability problem on the other side of the coin. However, in recent years, a steady increase in education spending on reforms and counter-reforms has led to more and more children having problems in learning and in life and, as a result, to an increase in educational difficulties at school and in families. This must make people sit up and take notice and requires a public commitment as to what schools can and must achieve.

Finally, the last thirty years have also changed educational science: While Hartmut von Hentig formulated his Socratic Oath against the background of a humanistic pedagogy, the benchmark is now empirical educational research. A renewal is important for this reason alone. It should be emphasised that neither the one nor the other of humanities pedagogy and empirical educational research is better or worse. Both form specific perspectives on education, and so it is the combination of these two approaches that matters.[17] Education requires both theoretical and empirical approaches. This leads to the emergence of a humanism as a guiding idea that has to prove itself in reality.[18] This demand has to be met for a professional oath in particular:[19] It may appear at first glance to be a theoretical construct, but empirical educational research provides the empirical proof, for example in the form of 'collective teacher efficacy'.

Other reasons could be cited; for instance, one could discuss the climate crisis, the North–South divide, or war and peace in the context of epochal challenges. However, the above considerations have already made it clear that every era requires a rethinking and reinterpretation of the Socratic Oath.

Notes

1 Cf. Zierer, K. (2019): Bildung, jetzt! In: *Scheidewege*, Heft 49, p. 372–387.

2 Cf. Pinker, S. (2018): *Enlightenment Now*. New York, und Rosling, H. (2018): *Factfulness*. London.

3 Cf. Klafki, W. (1996): *Neue Studien zur Bildungstheorie und Didaktik*. Weinheim.

4 Cf. Zierer, K. (2023): *Educating the COVID Generation*. London.

5 Cf. Wößmann, L. (2015): Die volkswirtschaftliche Bedeutung von Bildung. In: *Bundeszentrale für politische Bildung*, www.bpb.de/gesellschaft/bildung/zukunft-bildung/199450/volkswirtschaft-und-bildung (retrieved on 15.02.2023).

6 Cf. www.oecd.org/berlin/presse/hochstezeitfurhochqualifiziertetrotzbessererarbeits marktchancengeringerzuwachsbeiweiterfuhrendenabschlussenindeutschland.htm (retrieved on 26.02.2023).

7 Cf. on the concept of educational equity Zierer (2023), l. c.

8 Cf. Zierer, K. (2021c): Zwischen Dichtung und Wahrheit: Möglichkeiten und Grenzen von digitalen Medien im Bildungs-system. In: *Pädagogische Rundschau*, 4, p. 377–392.

9 Cf. Zierer, K. (2021d): Entgrenzung des Menschen durch Digitalisierung? In: *Zeitschrift für Pädagogik*, 1, p. 50–56.

10 Cf. Heidegger, M. (2001): *Sein und Zeit*. Tübingen.

11 Cf. Montag, C. (2018): *Homo Digitales*. Berlin.

12 Cf. Nida-Rümelin, J. & Zierer, K. (2020): Die Debatte über digitale Bildung ist entgleist. In: *NZZ*, p. 8.

13 Cf. Heidegger, M. (1954): *Die Frage nach der Technik*. Stuttgart.

14 Cf. Anders, G. (1980): *Die Antiquiertheit des Menschen*. Munich.

15 Anders (1980), l. c., p. 9. My Translation.

16 Nida-Rümelin & Zierer (2020), l. c., p. 9.

17 Cf. Zierer, K. (2009): Eklektik in der Pädagogik. Grundzüge einer gängigen Methode. In: *Zeitschrift für Pädagogik*, 6, p. 928–944.

18 Cf. Nida-Rümelin, N. & Zierer, K. (2017): Bildung in Deutschland vor neuen Herausforderungen. *Baltmannsweiler*, p. 23–30.

19 The combination of the two perspectives is one of the central points of criticism in Terhart (1987), l. c., and can be largely invalidated thanks to the further development of empirical approaches as well as a rapprochement of empirical educational research and humanistic pedagogy. Cf. Zierer (2009), l. c.

7 To whom is a commitment necessary and what must it contain?

In view of this mixed situation, I believe it is time to present a renewal of the Socratic Oath. It is a theoretically well-founded and empirically validated public commitment of teachers[1] to children, parents, colleagues, the educational public, society, and themselves.[2]

In the following, I explain and expound on the Socratic Oath as printed at the beginning of the book step by step. The justification of the individual points takes into account theoretical viewpoints and empirical findings in accordance with the completed argumentation. This is a justification, not a presentation of a possible implementation. For this, reference is made to further work at the relevant points.

> '*Let him that would move the world first move himself '.*[3]
>
> *Socrates*

Hartmut von Hentig placed his Socratic Oath under the following words, found in the *Apology of Socrates*:

> And I shall repeat the same words to every one whom I meet, young and old. . . . For know that this is the command of God. . . . Wherefore, O men of Athens, I say to you, do as Anytus bids or not as Anytus bids, and either acquit me or not; but whichever you do, understand that I shall never alter my ways, not even if I have to die many times.[4]

These lines are from Socrates' defence speech, in which he makes it clear that it is better to die than to act harmfully and that death is not a bad thing because it is in any case the absence of the evils that afflict life.[5] This serenity and confidence with which Socrates speaks at the hour of his death shows his piety, without which his life and philosophy cannot be understood.

Whether these words are still the best ones to initiate a professional oath for teachers today remains to be seen in view of the changes in society as a whole. Against the background of the results of empirical educational research, other passages seem to be just as suitable.

DOI: 10.4324/9781003439288-7

The quotation chosen for the renewal of the Socratic Oath can be found in many places and draws attention to two aspects of successful teachers: First, it points out that one must always remain inquisitive, always question oneself, see mistakes as opportunities, and not stand still. Second, it addresses the task of supporting, accompanying, and influencing both the individual and the community. Without this attitude, a teacher cannot be successful.

As a teacher, I commit myself to directing all my feelings, thoughts, and actions in my profession towards the well-being of the children entrusted to my care.

Hermann Giesecke criticises Hartmut von Hentig's Socratic Oath for not formulating a distinction between professional and private life.[6] This aspect is taken up in the renewal of the Socratic Oath, and it is made clear that it focuses on and is limited to the teaching profession. In addition, the areas of feeling, thinking, and acting are addressed since the latest professional research defines these aspects as central components of successful teachers.[7]

The term 'child' is not limited to a certain age but refers in the pedagogical context to those people whose education is supported and guided by other people through education and teaching.

To the children, I commit myself

- *to challenge and encourage each child according to his or her potential and level of development,*
- *not to leave any child behind or write them off, no matter what the reasons are,*
- *to take the failure of the children entrusted to me over and over again as an occasion for new ways of teaching,*
- *to see mistakes as an opportunity, not a flaw,*
- *to set challenges in the educational process so that under- and overstraining do not occur,*
- *to seek, pick up, and awaken motivations,*
- *to enter into dialogue again and again, to give and receive feedback, to ask questions and to listen,*
- *to assign subjects a serving function in the educational process,*
- *to address and stimulate all areas of the personality,*
- *to inspire confidence in the world and in oneself and to make it visible on a daily basis,*
- *to understand and shape the classroom and the school as a welcoming place,*
- *to provide an atmosphere and relationship that is respectful, free of fear, and educationally effective, and*
- *to stand up for the physical, mental, and spiritual integrity of the children entrusted to me.*

The children are the first and most important protagonists towards whom a commitment is necessary from a teacher's point of view. In addition, from the point of view of school theory and practice, there are the parents, the colleagues, and the educational public, as well as the educational administration, society as a whole, and also oneself. In Hartmut von Hentig's Socratic Oath, these aspects are listed without a systematic approach, which leads to a loss of clarity and comprehensibility.

The prioritisation of children is justified by the teacher's assumption of the constitutionally embodied educational mandate. The aforementioned double mandate associated with this, namely to bear responsibility for the education of the individual and the continuation of society, places the education of the individual at the centre in this context.

The points made in the Socratic Oath can be substantiated by a number of findings from empirical educational research, such as those summarised in lists of criteria for teaching quality.[8] From the perspective of educational science, it is undisputed that a positive culture of mistakes, in which mistakes are seen as important feedback for learners and teachers, is more conducive to learning and more effective for education than an atmosphere in which mistakes are seen as a flaw and cause fear. This requires target perspectives in teaching that are not too difficult and not too easy but that set the challenge by achieving an optimal fit between level of achievement on the one hand and level of demand on the other. With regard to the motivation of learners, an intrinsic (subject-related, e.g. interest in the subject) orientation is preferable to an extrinsic (non-subject-related, e.g. grade) one. Learning progress can be achieved in both cases, but the sustainability of educational success is clearly superior with intrinsic motivation and also avoids 'bulimic learning'. Forms of cooperation and exchange also enable the power of peers, that is, the importance of peers for education, to be taken up and used for learning and educational processes. All of the above presupposes that there is an intact teacher–pupil relationship in the classroom in which both sides approach each other with the necessary respect and interact with each other. Regular feedback and a dialogic structure of lessons are the way forward.

Another key point is that education encompasses more than subject knowledge and that subjects have a serving function. It is appropriate in this context to recall Howard Gardner's theory of multiple intelligences or Julian Nida-Rümelin's philosophy of a humane education.[9] In these approaches, it becomes clear that education as personality development includes social, emotional, motivational, physical, and many other elements in addition to cognitive elements. Any narrowing of humans to individual areas does not do them justice. The same applies to school subjects, each of which is important in its own right but only becomes educationally effective in combination with all other subjects.

Against this background, educational justice is a guiding pedagogical idea that unites three perspectives: first, an anthropological perspective according to which all children have a right to an education, regardless of their origin, appearance, religion, and the like; second, a pedagogical perspective, according to which all children are unique in terms of their possibilities for personality development, which highlights the importance of individualisation; and third, a sociological perspective, according to which the promotion of individuals can be particularly profitable for the community and is therefore justified. In the field of tension between these perspectives and in awareness of the corresponding teaching possibilities, the educational mandate is to be carried out by the teacher.[10]

Finally, this area also touches on a self-commitment on the part of the teachers to always approach children's learning and educational processes in relation to their own educational and teaching activities. This idea will be taken up again and explained in detail as the last point of the Socratic Oath.

One aspect requires special consideration at this point: standing up for the physical, mental, and spiritual integrity of the children entrusted to the teacher. Similar wording can already be found in Hartmut von Hentig's oath. The importance of this point is demonstrated by the atrocities at the Odenwald School, in which Hartmut von Hentig was involved because of his friendship with Gerold Becker. But they also demonstrate that a self-commitment alone is not enough to prevent crimes against children. The Socratic Oath leads here to a field of law that is indispensable in this context because misconduct in this regard will be legally prosecuted and lead to punishments under private, labour, and, if necessary, civil service law.

To the parents, I commit myself

- *to communicate on an equal footing and to establish an educational partnership,*
- *to understand the educational process of the children as a common task,*
- *not only to be prepared to talk to them on a regular basis, but also to actively seek contact with them, and*
- *to take their assessments of the children's educational success and progress seriously and to combine them with their own views.*

Parents are crucial for educational success. This is often discussed solely at the level of socioeconomic background and thus with a view to the parents' income, but the connections are more profound. For example, the way parents talk to their children, what they do together in their free time, how they trust their children and give them confidence are so closely linked to the children's educational process that it cannot succeed without successful parental involvement. The study 'The Early Catastrophe: The 30 Million Word Gap by Age 3' gets to the heart of this matter. It examined how many words children in precarious family situations hear in the first four years of life compared with children in well-off families: 15 million words to 45 million words – an immense difference. And it becomes even more serious when viewed qualitatively: Children from educationally advantaged backgrounds receive up to seven times more encouragement than discouragement, and children from educationally disadvantaged backgrounds hear a good twice as much discouragement as encouragement.[11] So the cards are on the table: Those who hear throughout their lives that they can't do something will have a very hard time later on.

There is no doubt that successful education at home is also influenced by financial possibilities. A good illustration of this can be found in empirical educational research, according to which children's reading performance is directly related to the number of books in the home.[12] However, this should not obscure the fact that there has to be more than just books: Reading aloud in the evening and talking together about what has been read is the decisive step that brings books to life.

On the one hand, these considerations show how important parents are for the educational success of their children, and on the other hand, they highlight that pedagogical support on the part of the schools helps parents to assume their responsibility in the first place. How many children leave home without break-fast, are not asked how they are doing when they come home, sit alone in their rooms for many hours a week, and the like? This assistance must not be seen by teachers as additional work alone, a prejudice that can be heard again and again. Certainly, working with parents can be time-consuming and exhausting, but successful cooperation with parents pays off above all in the classroom, leads to relief in everyday school life, and benefits the well-being of the child.

The basis for educational success in general and educational equity in particular is therefore successful cooperation between school and home. This is a proven result from empirical educational research.[13] In this respect, appropriate cooperation in the education system is indispensable and must therefore also be addressed in a professional oath.

To my colleagues, I commit myself

- *to share my experiences in education and teaching and to use them as a basis for collegial professionalisation,*
- *to share and reflect together on the mistakes made every day,*
- *to reflect back on successful moments in school and give mutual recognition and*
- *to allow everyone to have their own individual perspective on school and teaching while working towards a shared vision.*

In the 'Visible Learning' study, with over 2,100 meta-analyses – one of the largest data sets in empirical educational research[14] – the factor 'collective teacher efficacy' achieves one of the highest effects on learning performance. This term is used to summarise results that examine the influence of cooperation and exchange in the teaching staff on the academic performance of the learners and leads to a clear result: Effective teaching is not only a question of competence but also a question of attitude. If colleagues exchange ideas, find a common path, and develop a vision of a good school together, learners benefit the most. The shared vision of a school and the idea of what successful teaching looks like sustainably promote the learning performance of pupils. The teachers' collective expectation of effectiveness should not be understood as an opinion that must be shared by all and must not be questioned. Rather, it refers to mutual trust in overcoming barriers and limitations and to the common position that all learners in school may, indeed must, claim at least one year of learning progress for themselves. Only in this way will no child be left behind. The fact alone that every teacher teaches about 35,000 school hours in the course of their life and that none of these school hours is perfect makes it clear:[15] It is time to also see mistakes as an opportunity for professionalisation in colleges.

In view of these results, it is not so much the lone wolf as the team player who brings about teaching success. A culture of mistakes such as that demanded of students is therefore also important for teacher professionalisation and should be anchored in a professional oath.

To the educational public, I commit myself

- *to accept the educational mission and to implement it at all times,*
- *not only to impart knowledge and skills, but to focus on and promote all areas of the personality,*
- *to subordinate all subjects to the well-being of the child and thus to the educational mission,*
- *to be loyal, but not blind, to official requirements,*
- *to implement everything that is in the best interests of the child and to reject everything that is contrary to the best interests of the child,*
- *to critically question, and if necessary publicly accuse and reject, any interests and demands on schools and teaching that are not primarily in the best interests of the child, and*
- *to give a voice in public discourse to children and their right to education.*

At this point in the Socratic Oath, the educational mandate appears in explicit form. This is formulated in the constitutions of all the world's democracies. Although it differs in one passage or another, it is the basis for the school system. As a rule, teachers have to take an oath of office, especially if they are civil servants. In this respect, a special pedagogical obligation follows from this legal anchoring.

The background to these legal texts is that schools are institutions of society and for society. Teachers assume sovereign tasks through their school activities. They are mandated by the state, and their actions are legitimised, which requires a certain loyalty but which must not lead to blindness. The educational mandate is a special reflection of the double mandate: On the one hand, it is formulated from the point of view of the state as the mouthpiece of society, while on the other hand, it focuses on individuals and their educational processes. Consequently, whenever educational policy decisions have been made that run counter to the best interests of the child, the assumption of the educational mandate also requires that this be pointed out in all available places.[16]

This becomes clear when one reads individual constitutions. The Bavarian state constitution can serve as an example. Article 131 states:

(1)   Schools should not only impart knowledge and skills but also form heart and character.

(2)   The highest Bavarian educational goals are reverence for God; respect for religious conviction and human dignity; self-control; a sense of responsibility and a willingness to take responsibility; a willingness to help and an open-mindedness for all that is true, good, and beautiful; and a sense of responsibility for nature and the environment.

(3)   The pupils shall be educated in the spirit of democracy, in love for the Bavarian homeland and the German people, and in the spirit of reconciliation between nations.

(4)   The girls and boys are also to receive special instruction in baby care, child rearing, and home economics.

From an educational point of view, several points are noteworthy: First, the text of the law reveals a comprehensive understanding of education as formulated in a humanistic tradition. In this respect, education cannot be reduced to individual areas of the personality but encompasses human beings in all their possibilities. It follows directly from this that education should not be reduced to the cognitive alone but should also include moral, emotional, motivational, spiritual, and other similar facets.[17] Second, not a single subject is named in the cited article – not mathematics, not German, and not even the natural sciences – to designate the central domains of empirical educational research. Instead, there is a series of values: among others, respect for religious conviction and human dignity, a sense of responsibility and willingness to take on responsibility, a sense of responsibility for nature and the environment, an education in the spirit of democracy and in the spirit of international understanding; in view of the epochal challenges of our time, such as the COVID-19 pandemic, the climate crisis, and the war in Ukraine, a constitution could not be more topical. For teacher action, this means viewing subjects in a serving function. As important as they are, in the pedagogical context they have no end in themselves. Their purpose is rather to be subordinated to the education of children.

Without question, this passage of the Socratic Oath contains a number of moments of tension, as was exemplified by loyalty. Therefore, it is a mark of professionalism not to leave them out of account but to recognise them and to transform them into coherence in everyday school life. Living in dichotomies is one of the main tasks of teachers.[18]

To society, I commit myself

- *to see respect for the dignity of the human being as the basis and goal of school and teaching,*
- *to teach the principles of our democracy and to defend them in school and in the classroom,*
- *to see school as a place of reproduction and innovation of social values,*
- *to use my pedagogical freedom to place current issues at the centre of the school day, and*
- *to be not only reactive but also proactive towards the further development of our society.*

With this section of the Socratic Oath, the second perspective of the double mandate is brought fully into focus: responsibility for society. The points listed are derived from the foundations of democratic societies as enshrined in their constitutions, for example in Articles 1 to 20 of the Basic Law for the Federal Republic of Germany, and form the foundation for the educational mandate as it has already been explained. According to Jürgen Habermas, these foundations are not so much normative propositions as insights that follow the principle of universality.[19] First and foremost is Article 1: 'Human dignity is inviolable'. It is the duty of all state authority to respect and protect it. Teachers assume a sovereign task and are therefore particularly bound by this principle. In this respect, a corresponding obligation towards society is added to the above-mentioned obligation towards children in the interest of their physical, mental, and spiritual integrity. This once again emphasises the importance of this point and also that the Socratic Oath carries a legally binding force at this crucial point. Incidents like those at the Odenwald School must never happen again.

In addition, a theory of the school is taken up again because important implications for a professional oath arise from it against the background of the educational mission, which has its significance from the point of view of the individual and from the point of view of society. Thus, the task of schools is never only to pass on the existing cultural system but also to modernise. Schools are always a reflection of society, but at the same time, they are also a vision of how society should be in the future.[20]

To myself, I commit myself

- *to justify my actions at all times, to discuss them critically and constructively, and to reflect on them conscientiously,*
- *to regularly develop my professional, pedagogical and didactic competences,*
- *to regularly reflect on my professional attitudes and*
- *to always perform my function as a role model to the best of my knowledge and belief.*

In essence, it is almost trivial: teacher education – as a specific form of education – is to be understood as lifelong. It is a continuous process and does not end with the acquisition of a university degree, the passing of a state examination, or other such qualifications. Teachers are confronted throughout their lives with the challenge of coming to grips with changes to previously familiar framework conditions. Such changes in recent years include, above all, inclusion and digitalisation. These changes in society as a whole have an impact on schools and teaching and require teachers to constantly look at their professionalism, acquire competencies, and question their attitudes.

Apart from that, it should be noted that our living environment is constantly changing, and with it, educational concepts in families and schools. Against this background, teaching is subject to constant change. It may be true that a teacher has given the same lesson several times, but she has never given it to the same class. 'Panta rhei', as Heraclitus of Ephesus puts it,[21] means 'everything flows'. Just as you cannot step into the same river twice, you cannot give the same lesson twice; the learners have changed or are completely different, the social situation is different, the time of day and the spatial conditions are different, the lesson before was different, and you yourself are different. One's own professionalism and thus one's own competencies and attitudes are put to the test and change every day. So if there is something constant in school, it is change.

Facing up to this change is a central characteristic of professionalism and must therefore find its way into a renewal of the Socratic Oath. Research on teacher professionalism shows that the challenge this involves is best met in a team, as the remarks on collective efficacy have tried to make clear. The reality of teacher education has not yet consistently adopted this idea: Teachers are socialised too much as lone wolves; for example, teaching examinations are usually taken alone, even though teachers are supposed to work on teams later on. This is connected to a second problem: In many cases, the focus in teaching examinations for trainee teachers is on whether the lessons are error-free – as if there were a lesson that was error-free. In view of the studies on the professionalisation of teachers, the focus should be different and look more at the mistakes. Teachers teach about 35,000 lessons in their lifetime, none of which are perfect. So how do we deal with our mistakes? Do we close the door and hope that no one saw anything? The crucial questions therefore include: Where is the mistake? What didn't go so well and what could I have done better? What can I as a teacher learn from this for my next lessons? How can I use my mistakes to get into conversation with my colleagues? What is true of learners is equally true of teachers: The mistake is the motor of learning.[22]

After all, this is true not only in the present context but in all pedagogical encounters: Teachers take on a function as role models. Just as, in the words of Paul Watzlawick, one cannot not communicate,[23] one cannot not be a role model. The eyes of the learners follow a teacher day in and day out: when entering the classroom, during the lesson, when leaving the classroom, during the break, and when going home. Those who enter the teaching profession therefore need to be aware of their function as a role model, to question it again and again, and to perform it to the best of their knowledge and conscience.

I confirm what has been said by my willingness to be measured at all times against the standards that emanate from this commitment.

The conclusion of the Socratic Oath is the invitation to enter into a dialogue with all other actors in the education system. This is associated with an openness to criticism, provided that it is presented constructively. Feedback that constitutes a personal attack should not be included; at this point it is not about condemning but about an exchange on the best possible education for learners and for society as a whole. An exception to this is the misconduct that has already been mentioned several times, such as that which occurred at the Odenwald School and which must lead directly to private, labour, and, if necessary, civil service law proceedings.

As Hartmut von Hentig formulated at the time, the Socratic Oath could be spoken when teachers are presented with their certificates of employment – after it has already been thematised in the first and second stages of teacher education and before it is used again and again as an impetus for discussion in the course of daily teaching and lifelong professionalisation. If the epochal challenges cannot be solved by education alone, it is equally certain that they cannot be mastered for the good of humanity without education.

Notes

1 One criticism of the Socratic Oath by Hentig (1991), l. c., was that he only argued from his experience, cf. Giesecke (1997), l. c., p. 268. In the present reformulation, both theoretical considerations and empirical results are deliberately cited as justification. Cf. also Terhart (1987), l. c., p. 794.
2 Giesecke (1997), l. c., criticises that Hentig (1991), l. c., only takes the perspective of the teacher and is thus undifferentiated in his statement. The subdivision into the central protagonists for educational processes corrects this objection.
3 Platon (1924): *Euthyphron*, 10B. Oxford.
4 Platon (1892), l. c., 30A.
5 Cf. Figal (2001), l. c., p. 52.
6 Cf. Giesecke (1997), l. c.
7 Cf. Hattie & Zierer (2018), l. c.
8 Cf. Brophy, J.E. (1999): *Teaching*. Genf; Helmke, A. (2014): *Unterrichtsqualität und Lehrerprofessionalität. Diagnose, Evaluation und Verbesserung des Unterrichts*. Stuttgart; Hattie & Zierer (2018), l. c.
9 Cf. Gardner, H. (1983): *Frames of Mind – The Theory of Multiple Intelligences*. New York; Nida-Rümelin & Zierer (2017), l. c.; Zierer, K. (2018): Bildung. In: *Pädagogische Rundschau*, 72(3), p. 341–361.

10 Cf. Zierer (2023), l. c.
11 Cf. Hart, B. & Risley, T.R. (2003): The Early Catastrophe: The 30 Million Word Gap by Age 3. In: *American Educator*, p. 4–9.
12 Cf. The international comparative studies on reading literacy, e.g., Hußmann, A. et al. (2017): *IGLU 2016*. Münster, here p. 21.
13 Cf. Hattie & Zierer (2018), l. c., p. 105f.
14 Cf. Hattie, J. (2023): *Visible Learning – The Sequel*. London.
15 Cf. Hattie & Zierer (2020), l. c., p. 295.
16 Helmut Fend points to this tension in his theory of the school. Cf. Fend (2008), l. c.
17 Cf. Gardner (1983), l. c., and Nida-Rümelin & Zierer (2017), l. c.
18 Classic dichotomies in pedagogy are freedom and coercion, closeness and distance, leading and letting grow. Cf. Litt, T. (1929): *Führen oder Wachsenlassen*. Leipzig.
19 Cf. Habermas, J. (1983): *Moralbewusstsein und kommunikatives Handeln*. Frankfurt, p. 53–126.
20 Helmut Fend describes this idea with the words 'reproduction' and 'innovation'. Cf. Fend (2008), l. c.
21 Cf. Diels, H. (2008): *Poetarum philosophorum fragmenta*. Berlin.
22 Cf. Hattie (2023), l. c.
23 Cf. Watzlawick, P., Beavin, J. & Jackson, D. (2016): *Menschliche Kommunikation*. Bern, p. 58f.

8 What happens next?

When my article on the Socratic Oath, 'What is a good teacher?', appeared in the *Neue Zürcher Zeitung* on 21 March 2022, it did not take long before I received the first messages. They ranged (as they always do when one takes a public stand) from approval to rejection. The comments in social media also reflect this impression, although comment columns, tweets, and the like are usually less expressions of deeper reflection than of fleeting thoughts.

Criticism is important. It is the motor of development and of the search for insights. Criticism is therefore always welcome. But not all feedback is criticism in this sense. In many cases, feedback is personal. John Hattie wrote me back in a message in which I had described a corresponding situation one day: 'We were taught to criticise ideas, not people'.

With this in mind, I do not wish to respond below to comments that become personal. Instead, I would like to take up the points that have helped me in my reflections on the Socratic Oath.

If we take this criticism and look back at the arguments I have made, we can derive in individual aspects what the Socratic Oath is not or what it is in essence. Possible misinterpretations can be avoided from the outset in this way.

First, the Socratic Oath is not absolute in the sense that what has been said once is valid forever. On the contrary, the Socratic Oath is an attempt to provide an orientation that is to be questioned and reflected upon anew by each generation. In this sense, it is an invitation to engage in a dialogue about one's own professionalism. For example, the reaction to missing a certain value can be seen as exactly what was said before: entering the conversation about what constitutes education today.

Second, the Socratic Oath is visionary. It is not uncommon for the reaction to the Socratic Oath to be, 'Who's going to do it? No one can always keep these commitments'. That is undoubtedly true. But the alternative would be to formulate a Socratic Oath that could be kept by everyone at all times. In this way, it would fall into the trivial and would no longer have any meaning. Thus, the Socratic Oath is not an attempt to formulate a minimum standard but should be understood as a maximum standard. It contains a vision of how

DOI: 10.4324/9781003439288-8

teachers should act on a daily basis in order to have a basis for reflecting on how they acted on a daily basis.

Third, the Socratic Oath is meant to be not a prerequisite for taking up a teaching position but a consequence of it. This derives from the evidence-based insight that successful teacher action is always a matter of attitude. Consequently, it is part of professionalisation not only to care about one's own competency development but also to scrutinise one's own cosmos of values and to relate them to scientific results.

Fourth, the Socratic Oath should be seen in and of itself without legal consequences. It is essentially a self-commitment. Without question, however, misconduct in individual fields of professional teacher action, which are already addressed in the Socratic Oath, can lead to consequences under private, labour, and, if applicable, civil service law.

And fifth, while the Socratic Oath stands on its own, it also interacts with other commitments. A common reaction to the Socratic Oath is: 'Why should I do something if the others don't do something too? Only when everyone takes an oath and keeps it do I feel compelled to do the same'. As understandable as this argument is, it is misleading, for a teacher's self-commitment must not be subject to the condition of another commitment. It must first stand for itself; otherwise it loses its meaning and its power. This does not mean that all other actors in the education system and beyond must also make a commitment to educational success and social cohesion. But a professional oath must first be understood as a self-commitment for its own sake. In this sense, a professional oath has holistic features. If the Socratic Oath were to be placed under the condition of another oath, it would no longer be an oath. For a self-commitment that is dependent on something else is no longer a self-commitment but the consequence of that something else. In view of these considerations, however, it is worthwhile for learners, parents, the educational public, and society to think about aspects of an educational oath that can manifest the unity of a vision of the future of education for society as a whole.

Here are just a few thoughts in these directions: On the part of the children, there is the obligation to accept the teachers' offer and to be open to it. It is equally important that children conscientiously take charge of their own development, question themselves, reflect on their own learning process, and see mistakes as opportunities. On the part of the parents, there is the obligation to accept the educational partnership with the school. Thus, parents are responsible for what happens or does not happen at home. Success at school in particular and success in education in general is never the responsibility of a single person but always the result of the successful interaction of all those involved. On the part of the educational public, there is an obligation to give the field of education the attention it deserves with regard to the individual but also with regard to the community. This requires an attitude of shaping and not just one of administration. It is also essential to give the actors trust and confidence; those who want to avoid every mistake on the spot or sanction them if necessary take away creativity from the education system, which is so important for education. And finally, on the part of society, there is the obligation to allow debates about education and to place them at the centre of attention. For far too long, many countries did not debate education as an overall societal goal; for example, Germany has rested on its heritage as the land of poets and thinkers and overlooked, even negated, the need for a fundamental discourse on education. The empirical data on the achievement level of learners and also the epochal challenges make it clear that further development of the education system is indispensable.[1]

Against this background, it is the following three-step process that emerges in the face of a renewal of the Socratic Oath:

Create structures, strengthen people, professionalise teaching.

This three-step process is so often thought of from the front and thus from the outside in, with the following result: First, the structures are changed, which always involves a great deal of financial effort and creates the feeling on the part of all those involved that they are not being taken along. Thus, these reforms already falter at the level of the people; they hardly ever reach and change the teaching. The digitisation campaign of recent years is one example of this among many others, and once again Germany serves as an example: Of the five billion euros already made available by the federal government in 2019, not even 10 per cent had been spent by the beginning of 2022 – despite the COVID-19 crisis.[2]

The results of empirical educational research, however, have proven for several years, if not decades, that the aforementioned three-step process must be reversed, or at least followed in steps. Without a focus on teaching, almost all educational reforms fizzle out.

This approach is linked to the perspective of why. The education system is not only changed because money is available or external constraints exist, but reforms are initiated that start from the child and lead towards the child. In this way, schools and thus education can be rethought and changed in a sustainable way.

In this respect, it makes sense to start by focusing on teachers and formulating a professional oath. From here, a fundamental debate on the future of schools and education can be initiated. Teachers have one of the most important professions, perhaps even the most important profession in our society. They not only influence whether a person's 15,000 hours of schooling are enjoyable or not. It depends on them and their professionalism how people are educated, how their personalities develop, how a country's democracy stands, and how a country's economic power develops.

Education is the highest good of a society. It is high time that all countries and all societies around the world openly debated education again. The Socratic Oath can and will be an impetus here. In the words of John F. Kennedy: 'There is only one thing more expensive in the long run than education – no education'.

Notes

1 Cf. Zierer (2023), l. c.
2 Cf. www.spiegel.de/panorama/bildung/digitalpakt-schule-nach-zweieinhalb-jahren-sind-nicht-einmal-zehn-prozent-der-gelder-angekommen-a-0accb6a3-0e17-4a9c-97a8-e03e83e5b955 (retrieved on 02.05.2022).

Literature

www.bundestag.de/resource/blob/585474/a98216050ea29dcda7 26f464caa1f236/WD-3-368-18-pdf-data.pdf (retrieved on 24.02.2023).

www.comp.nus.edu.sg/~tantc/personal/pledge.html (retrieved on 24.02.2023).

www.derwesten.de/wirtschaft/nutzer-klagen-iphone-6-plus-verbiegt-sich-in-hosentasche-id9861181.html (retrieved on 05.02.2023).

www.diplomatie.gouv.fr/en/french-foreign-policy/human-rights/freedom-of-religion-or-belief/article/national-tribute-to-the-memory-of-samuel-paty-speech-by-emmanuel-macron (retrieved on 21.02.2023).

www.educationtoday.com.au/news-detail/Do-We-Need-a-Renewal-of-the-Socratic-Oath-5599 (retrieved on 24.02.2023).

www.encyclopedia.com/history/dictionaries-thesauruses-pictures-and-press-releases/teachers-loyalty-oath (retrieved on 25.02.2023).

www.mekulipress.com/betimi-i-mesuesit/ (retrieved on 24.02.2023).

www.ndtv.com/education/teachers-day-kalams-10-oaths-for-tea chers-1746387 (retrieved on 24.02.2023).

www.oaj.fi/en/education/ethical-principles-of-teaching/comenius-oath-for-teachers/ (retrieved on 24.02.2023).

www.oecd.org/berlin/presse/hochstezeitfurhochqualifiziertetrotzbessererarbeits marktchancengeringerzuwachsbeiweiterfuhrendenabschlussenindeutschland.htm (retrieved on 26.02.2023).

www.spiegel.de/panorama/bildung/digitalpakt-schule-nach-zwei-einhalb-jahren-sind-nicht-einmal-zehn-prozent-der-gelder-angekommen-a- 0accb6a3-0e17-4a9c-97a8-e03e83e5b955 (abgerufen am 02.02.2023).

www.spiegel.de/politik/deutschland/gerhard-schroeder-ueber- lehrer-doch-keine-faulen-saecke-a-3231b394-af98-4ab7-8131-e08ac1557fe0 (retrieved on 21.02.2023).

www.teacherph.com/2016-oath-taking-professional-teachers/ (abgerufen am 24.02.2023).

Anders, G. (1980): *Die Antiquiertheit des Menschen*. München.

Aristoteles (1956): *Nikomachische Ethik. Band 6 der Reihe "Aristoteles – Werke"*. Berlin.

Aristoteles (1999): *Rhetorik*. Stuttgart.

Baumert, J. & Kunter, M. (2006): Stichwort: Professionelle Kompetenz von Lehrkräften. In: *Zeitschrift für Erziehungswissenschaft*, Heft 9, S. 469–452.

Blömeke, S., Kaiser, G. & Lehmann, R. (Hrsg.) (2010): *TEDS-M 2008: Professionelle Kompetenz und Lerngelegenheiten angehender Primarstufenlehrkräfte im internationalen Vergleich*. Münster.

Bollnow, O.F. (2009): *Das Wesen der Stimmungen*. Würzburg.

Brezinka, W. (1986): *Erziehung in einer wertunsicheren Gesellschaft*. München.

Brinkmann, M. & Rödel, S.S. (2021): Ethos im Lehrerberuf – Haltung zeigen und Haltung üben. In: *Journal für LehrerInnenbildung*, Heft 3, S. 42–62.

Brophy, J.E. (1999): *Teaching*. Genf.

Diels, H. (2008): *Poetarum philosophorum fragmenta*. Berlin.

Drahmann, M. & Cramer, C. (2019): Vermutungen über das Lehrerethos – Revisited. In: Cramer, C. & Oser, F.: *Ethos – Interdisziplinäre Perspektiven auf den Lehrerinnen- und Lehrerberuf*. Münster, S. 15–36.

Fend, H. (2008): *Neue Theorie der Schule*. Wiesbaden.

Figal, G. (2001): Sokrates. In: *Große Philosophen*. Darmstadt, S. 49–61.

Gardner, H. (1983): *Frames of Mind – The Theory of Multiple Intelligences*. New York.

Gardner, H., Csíkszentmihályi, M. & Damon, W. (2005): *Good Work*. Stuttgart.

Giesecke, H. (1997): *Die pädagogische Beziehung*. Weinheim.

Habermas, J. (1983): *Moralbewusstsein und kommunikatives Handeln*. Frankfurt.

Habermas, J. (1989): Heidegger – Werk und Weltanschauung. In: Farias, V. (Hrsg.): *Heidegger und der Nationalsozialismus*. Frankfurt, S. 11–37.

Habermas, J. (1995): *Theorie des kommunikativen Handelns*. Frankfurt.

Hart, B. & Risley, T.R. (2003): The Early Catastrophe: The 30 Million Word Gap by Age 3. In: *American Educator*, S. 4–9.

Hattie, J. (2013): *Visible Learning for Teachers*. London.

Hattie, J. (2023): *Visible Learning – The Sequel*. London.

Hattie, J. & Zierer, K. (2018): *10 Mindframes for Visible Learning*. London.

Hattie, J. & Zierer, K. (2020): *Visible Learning Unterrichtsplanung*. Baltmannsweiler.

Heidegger, M. (1954): *Die Frage nach der Technik*. Stuttgart.

Heidegger, M. (2001): *Sein und Zeit*. Tübingen.

Helmke, A. (2014): *Unterrichtsqualität und Lehrerprofessionalität. Diagnose, Evaluation und Verbesserung des Unterrichts*. Stuttgart.

Hentig, H. (1991): Der neue Eid. In: *DIE ZEIT*, Nr. 39.

Hentig, H. v. (2016): *Noch immer mein Leben. Erinnerungen und Kommentare aus den Jahren 2005 bis 2015*. Berlin.

Hußmann, A. et al. (2017): *IGLU 2016*. Münster.

Klafki, W. (1996): *Neue Studien zur Bildungstheorie und Didaktik*. Weinheim.

Kunter, M., Baumert, J., Blum, W., Klusmann, U., Krauss, S. & Neubrand, M. (Hrsg.) (2011): *Professionelle Kompetenz von Lehrkräften. Ergebnisse des Forschungsprogramms COACTIV*. Münster.

Litt, T. (1929): *Führen oder Wachsenlassen*. Leipzig.

Lütjen, J. (2013): *Das Bildungswegmodell zur Rehabilitation der sokratischen Mäeutik*. Hamburg.

Montag, C. (2018): *Homo Digitales*. Berlin.

Nida-Rümelin, J. & Zierer, K. (2020): Die Debatte über digitale Bildung ist entgleist. In: *NZZ*, 08.06.2020, S. 8.

Nida-Rümelin, N. & Zierer, K. (2017): *Bildung in Deutschland vor neuen Herausforderungen*. Baltmannsweiler.

Pant, H.A., Stanat, P., Schroeders, U., Roppelt, A., Siegle, T. & Pöhlmann, C. (2013): *IQB- Ländervergleich 2012*. Münster.

Pinker, S. (2018): *Enlightenment Now*. New York.

Platon (1892): *The Apology of Socrates*. Oxford.

Platon (1924): *Euthyphron*. Oxford.

Rosling, H. (2018): *Factfulness*. London.

Rutter, M. et al. (1980): *15 000 Stunden. Schulen und ihre Wirkung auf die Kinder*. Weilheim.

Rychner, M. (2015): Der sokrati- sche Eid, professionstheoretisch gelesen. In: *Journal für LehrerInnenbildung*, Heft 3, S. 42–46.

Sinek, S. (2009): *Start with Why – How Great Leaders Inspire Everyone to Take Action*. New York.

Störig, H.J. (1998): *Kleine Weltgeschichte der Philosophie*. Frankfurt.

Terhart, E. (1987): Vermutungen über das Lehrerethos. In: *Zeitschrift für Pädagogik*, Heft 6, S. 787–804.

Watzlawick, P., Beavin, J. & Jackson, D. (2016): *Menschliche Kommunikation*. Bern.

Weber, M. (1992): *Politik als Beruf*. Stuttgart.

Wiersing, E. (2020): *Hartmut von Hentig*. Bielefeld.

Wilber, K. (2002): *Eros, Kosmos, Logos – Eine Jahrtausend-Vision*. Frankfurt.

Wößmann, L. (2015): Die volkswirtschaftliche Bedeutung von Bildung. In: *Bundeszentrale für politische Bildung*, www.bpb.de/gesellschaft/bildung/zukunftbildung/199450/volkswirtschaft-und-bildung (abgerufen am 15.03.2022).

Wößmann, L. et al. (2020): Bildung in der Corona-Krise: Wie haben die Schulkinder die Zeit der Schulschließungen verbracht, und welche Bildungs- maßnahmen befürworten die Deutschen? *ifo Schnelldienst*, Nr. 09.

Zierer, K. (2009): Eklektik in der Pädagogik. Grundzüge einer gängigen Methode. In: *Zeitschrift für Pädagogik*, Heft 6, S. 928–944.

Zierer, K. (2015): Educational Expertise: The Concept of 'Mind Frames' as an Integrative Model for Professionalisation in Teaching. In: *Oxford Review of Education*, 41(6), S. 782–798, http://dx.doi.org/10.1080/03054985.2015.1121140 (abgerufen am 24.03.2022).

Zierer, K. (2018): Bildung. In: *Pädagogische Rundschau*, 72(3), S. 341–361.

Zierer, K. (2019): Bildung, jetzt! In: *Scheidewege*, Heft 49, S. 372–387.

Zierer, K. (2020): Stichwort Haltungen. In: *weiter bilden*, Heft 3, S. 10–11.

Zierer, K. (2021a): Erhard Wiersing: Hartmut von Hentig – Ein Essay zu Leben und Werk. In: *Zeitschrift für Pädagogik*, Heft 6, S. 972–976.

Zierer, K. (2021c): Zwischen Dichtung und Wahrheit: Möglichkeiten und Grenzen von digitalen Medien im Bildungssystem. In: *Pädagogische Rundschau*, Heft 4, S. 377–392.

Zierer, K. (2021d): Entgrenzung des Menschen durch Digitalisierung? In: *Zeitschrift für Pädagogik*, Heft 1, S. 50–56.

Zierer, K. (2023): *Educating the COVID Generation*. London.

Zierer, K., Lachner, C., Tögel, J. & Weckend, D. (2018): Teacher Mindframes from an Educational Science Perspective. In: *Education Sciences*, 8(4), 209, https://doi.org/10.3390/educsci8040209.

Index

Note: Numbers in *italics* indicate figures on the corresponding page. Numbers with an "n" indicate a note on the corresponding page.

Printed in the United States
by Baker & Taylor Publisher Services